POSTMISTRESS

MORA, WASH.

1914–1915

JOURNAL ENTRIES AND PHOTOGRAPHS

OF FANNIE TAYLOR

EDITED BY

JACILEE WRAY & DOREEN TAYLOR

Postmistress—Mora, Wash. 1914-1915: Journal Entries and Photographs of Fannie Taylor

Edited by Jacilee Wray & Doreen Taylor

Copyright © 2006
Northwest Interpretive Association

Published by
Northwest Interpretive Association
164 South Jackson Street, Seattle, WA 98104
www.nwpubliclands.org

ISBN-10: 0-914019-57-0
ISBN-13: 978-0-914019-57-2

Printed in the United States of America

Northwest Interpretive Association is a 501$_c$3 nonprofit corporation. Our purpose is to provide for the enhanced enjoyment and understanding of visitors to public lands in our areas of operation located in Washington, Oregon, Montana, Idaho, and California.

Book and Cover Design by Ben Nechanicky

CONTENTS

FOREWORD

This book provides a unique view into one of the last settled areas in the continental United States, the "West End" of the Olympic Peninsula. The area is remote, isolated from the rest of Washington by the rugged Olympic Mountains. Early settlers reached the area by boat and Indian ocean-going canoe more frequently than overland routes, and the settlement of Mora near the mouth of the Quillayute River was an important port of call on this remote coast. This small settlement grew from a trading post to a small community with a salmon cannery, school, store, and post office. Fannie Taylor documented the community through her journals and photographs, providing a view of life at this remote edge of the Olympic Peninsula.

Fannie Taylor's position as Postmistress placed her in contact with everyone in the community, settlers and Quileute alike, and she wrote of those day to day contacts and events. In addition, she was an accomplished photographer, with hundreds of her photos surviving today. As a result, her journals give a unique insight into the character of the entire community, and matched with photos of place and time are a reflection of the history of the West End that can be enjoyed by all.

Larry Burtness
Project Manager
Northwest Olympic Peninsula
Community Museum Project

ACKNOWLEDGMENTS

First and foremost I thank Doreen Taylor. If it were not for her preservation of the diaries and photographs, this wonderful resource would be long gone. Doreen donated the diaries and most of Fannie's photographs to Olympic National Park in 1995. Doreen was married to Ken Taylor, the son of Lloyd, who was Fannie and WF Taylor's son. Doreen's kindness in sharing these and all of her recollections, as well as her assistance with the editing has been invaluable.

I am indebted to Ed Maupin who first told me I should talk to Ken Taylor, unfortunately by the time I got around to it, Ken had passed away, but that is how I met Doreen. Ed has also provided reviews of the manuscript and given me much information. Ed Maupin is the grandson of Mina Smith who lived on the Dickey, upriver from the Taylor's, and is the only person I have found that remembers meeting Fannie Taylor. Ed's own photograph collection, his knowledge of the Quillayute Prairie homesteaders and their relationships was invaluable and added much detail to Fannie's diaries. I would also like to thank Ed's nephew, Jeff Reyes, who took great interest in this project and assisted with research through the Peninsula College internship program.

I am very thankful for the memories of family members of some of the area's early settlers — the Maxfield sisters, Eleanor Thornton and Anita Tuttle; the Palmer sisters, Elsie Motteler and Betty Palmer; Eleanor "Toots" Wirick; Betty and Art Munson; Jack and June Olson; Jean James; Chris Morganroth III, Aha Blip (Elsa Schmidt), Lela Mae Morganroth, Gary Peterson, Ron Shearer, Kristian Kofoed, Sue Payne, Polly (Rixon) Polhamus, Missy (Elizabeth) Barlow, Tom Rixon, and Del and Muriel Huggins. They all helped with the history and in identifying photographs.

I want to give Larry Burtness from the U.W. Libraries Community Museum a special thank you for writing the foreword and for sharing several relevant historic documents with me. Some of Fannie's photographs are featured on the Community Museum website that was launched in October, 2006. I also want to thank Matthew Sneddon from the University of Washington Community Museum project for rescanning many of the Taylor photographs at a higher resolution.

I am grateful to Sue Goss for her index of the Taylor collection at the Forks Museum that came from the Museum and Arts Center in the

Sequim — Dungeness Valley. I am also very appreciative of the Museum and Arts Center for sharing some of the panoramic photos that Doreen Taylor had donated to them earlier and to photographer Robert Cooper who made prints of the panoramic images for this project.

I feel very lucky to have met and interviewed two descendants of the Morse family, who are prominent in Fannie's diaries; Nell Morse's daughter Margaret Cotter and Hugh Morse's son Bob Morse were able to help identify Morse family members and fill in many missing pieces.

Thanks also to Carolyn Marr for her additional information on Sam Morse.

I am grateful to Kathy Monds and the Clallam County Historical Society for including some of Fannie Taylor's history in the Museum at the Carnegie.

Thank you to Heather Hennum for her many hours scanning Taylor photos back in 1995. I'd also like to thank Peninsula College anthropology instructor Michele Laubenheimer and her student interns: Leilani Alberti, Angie Berglund, Roni Campbell, Kittie Dunn, Diane Duncan, Melanie Finley, Crickett Heassler, Steve Marshall, Elissa Melodyn, Bonnie Richardson, and Belynda Weideman. Special acknowledgement and appreciation goes to Christina Williams and Bernice Byrne for volunteering so much of their time to assist me.

Finally thank you to everyone who read the manuscript and encouraged me by telling me of its importance and that it should be published without changing Fannie's voice.

I have never been so taken by someone's life as I have Fannie Taylor's. This book will expand the recognition of this woman's life on the early Northwest Coast so that others may enjoy it as well.

Jacilee Wray

PREFACE

In a remote part of the Olympic Peninsula there was once a tiny seaport community called Mora,[1] located a mile from the mouth of the Quillayute River, at its confluence with the Dickey River or *Dickodochtedar.*[2] Across the Quillayute River to the south, the Quileute Indian Reservation at LaPush was established by Executive Order in 1889 to accommodate the people indigenous to the 700,000 acres of surrounding territory.

LaPush from James Island

The first homestead in the Mora area was that of Frank T. Balch in 1869. Balch managed the first post office, established in 1891, which he named Boston. Krång Olof (K.O.) Erikson homesteaded nearby in 1888 and purchased the Balch homestead in 1893. In 1900 Erikson renamed the location Mora after his home in Sweden. From 1898 until 1909 K.O. and his wife managed the post office. Erikson leased the store to W.F. and Fannie Ellen Taylor in 1908. The Taylors had moved to Washington from South Dakota, where W.F. worked for the railroad.

In November 1909 the Taylor's acquired the homestead of James B. Dodge at what came to be called Taylor Point.[3] Four families had homesteads in this area: [T.F.] Rixon, [Walter] Newbert, [George] Yates, and [W.F.] Taylor. They began their own school district, and built a schoolhouse by fall of 1910. The year before, the Taylor children, Lloyd (5/7/1894) and Laurel or "Tealie" (11/7/1897) attended the Mora school. The following year they moved out to the homestead and Lloyd and Tealie attended school there. The school district only lasted until 1913 and the Taylor Point place became a cabin retreat, while the family lived at Mora.

Taylor Point cabin or the "ranche"

Fannie Taylor took over the postmistress position from Minnie Erickson on April 1, 1909, and continued as postmistress until 1924 when Tealie took the job, while Fannie taught school in Arizona for the Indian Service. Fannie again became postmistress at Mora in 1937 until September 30, 1942, when the post office was discontinued as a result of the area being purchased under the Public Works Administration, to be added to Olympic National Park in 1953.

The diaries of Fannie Taylor, written from 1914 to 1922, had been preserved by her family and donated to Olympic National Park by Doreen Taylor, Fannie's grandson's wife. At Mora Fannie operated the store and overnight accommodations and served some meals, as well as serving as Postmistress. She also worked for the Indian Service as teacher at LaPush in 1919, 1922, and 1923. In her diaries Fannie describes the day to day activities of community life at Mora, as well as the vivid descriptions of her homestead at Taylor Point, or "the Ranche" as she called it — sometimes spelling it with the "e" at the end. She also kept a commentary of interactions with road builders, miners, neighbors-Quileute and non-Indians, the stage and mail drivers, and the occasional tourist. Fannie was an aspiring photographer,

Lloyd and Tealie Taylor

and her photos, combined with her journal entries, are a wonderful portrait of the time period.

This project, however gratifying, is fraught with unanswered questions, as Fannie's journal entries only span a brief time period, and her photos are unlabeled — although they are numbered for an index system, the index itself has not been found. The photos have been identified when possible by using information in her journals, supplemented by archival documents from the National Archives, Brigham Young University, Museum and Arts Center in the Sequim — Dungeness Valley, census records, historic newspapers, as well as talking with many local residents. Unfortunately, it seems that all those who would have remembered Fannie are now gone. The information available is still tremendous, and it is with a reverence for Fannie Ellen Taylor that we have brought these photos and words to the readers, which portray a time capsule of life on the Washington coast in the early 1900s.

INTRODUCTION

Fannie Taylor moved to Mora, Washington during a time when the Indian Agent and schoolteacher had major roles in restricting and regulating tribal lifeways, in other words, attempting to assimilate the Quileute into the dominant culture. Not only did these "supervisors" enforce mandatory schooling, and control government rations, they also heavily restricted traditional ceremonies such as the potlatch and Shaker[4] meetings.

In 1905 the Neah Bay Indian Agency Superintendent, Edwin Minor wrote a "Notice to Shakers:"

> You are hereby permitted to hold meetings on Quileute Reservation under the following condition:

> On Sundays not longer than three hours at one time and on Wednesday evenings no longer than two hours at one time. With the following REGULATIONS to be observed:

> 1st Keep windows or a door open during all meetings.

> 2nd Use only one bell to give signals. Not continuous ringing.

> 3rd Do not admit school children at night meetings (Minor 1905).

Then on December 13, 1905, Edwin Minor wrote to the tribal police officer, Luke Hobucket [To-husk], a Quileute tribal member, that

> It has been reported to me that there are some women who are violating the Rules for holding Shaker meetings, and that they shake at all times of the day and night.

> You will therefore tell the women quietly to stop shaking at any other times than the times specified in the rules that I issued last summer. If they do not stop, after you have asked them in a quiet way, you will lock them up untill [sic] they agree to stop.

Shaking for the sick must not be allowed. Before you make any arrests under this order, you should report to Mr. Reagan [Albert B. Reagan, Indian Agency teacher at LaPush] and get his advice. We do not want any trouble in this matter if it is possible to avoid it; but that "continual and private shaking" must be stopped. Report what you do (Minor 1905a).

Reagan wrote to agent Minor that he had been asked by Quileute, Henry Hobucket "in the strongest terms to cease enforcing the regulations direct from your office," stating that they were not enforced at Neah Bay. "I told him that we would enforce the regulations until we got a letter from you withdrawing them" (Reagan 1906).

Superintendent Minor wrote back to Reagan:

We must do the best we can trying to carry out the policy of the Commissioner of Indian Affairs. The conduct of the Shakers is well known at the Indian Office. Good judgment and patience must be exercised in dealing with them, and as the honorable commissioner says, "Try to show them a better way" (Minor 1906).

The Shaker religious practices were still carried out in 1909 at LaPush, as noted in the Quileute Tribe's newspaper:

[The Shaker Religion] is said to be foolish by one of the officials in the Indian office but no rule to prevent it was made as the Indians claim their rights in accordance with the United States Constitution (Quileute Independent 1909).

In 1906 the potlatch was also severely restricted as described in a letter to Superintendent Minor from Reagan.

The Neah Bays, the Shaker missionary people and Jack Ward's people have come and gone. For two weeks practically no one struck a lick of work, feasting being the order of the day. This culminated in Jack Ward's so called wedding feast in which the Neah Bays gave to the people the several boxes of hard biscuit crackers which they had brought with them. The Quileutes gave a few bunches of basket straw and some dishes (the presents were given to Mrs. Ward with my permission, Jack Ward stating that you said that it would be alright to give his wife wedding presents). Then the Quileutes handed around money and basket straw to the Neah Bay visitors. This they said was given to pay for the crackers and that you had given them permission to do it. I was not consulted at all in the money and basket straw giving to the Neah Bays. Mr. Ward and Thos. Payne furnished most of the money (Reagan 1906).

In 1907 Reagan wrote to the new Superintendent and physician at Neah Bay, Dr. C.L. Woods:

> Being asked the permission to "pay" for some more crackers for a feast to be given by the Queets Indians, I respectfully ask: Shall I allow the Indians to pay publicly in money and goods for the crackers furnished at their feasts? (Reagan 1907).

In May, Superintendent Woods wrote to Reagan that he has

> ...learned that a feast on the order of a "pot-latch" is contemplated by the Quileute Indians on the 4th of July.... If such is the case, you will please stop all further proceedings and inform the parties concerned that it will not be allowed. It is said that the celebration is to be in honor of the daughter of Dan White [Ida (*Chutsk*) born circa 1895] who is to be about "that age" on the 4th (Woods 1907).

Possibly Quileute homes on the north side of the Quillayute River.

Quileute boys, dog, and cow

Probably Bill Hudson and wife Demer
Cole Hudson

Game Warden Howeattle, probably
Arthur, on Bird Island (*do-si-aht-si-tah*
"place where you go to get petrels")

Unidentified Quileute schoolgirls

Daniel White [*Kwalsoob*], and his wife Evalina, had a cabin on the slough of the Quillayute[5] River at Mora. They also had a cabin and smokehouse at the confluence of the East and West Dickey near the Mina Smith homestead. Mina's daughter, Dorothy Smith told her son Ed Maupin that she could hear them [Daniel & Evalina White] greet the morning by chanting and reciting a prayer to an Indian spirit (Maupin 2003).

On May 29, 1907, Quileute tribal member George Woodruff wrote a letter to the Indian Agency:

Just recently in the post office at Mora in the presence of Mr. K.O. Erickson and

George Woodruff

myself it was the first part of last week, Henry Hudson [Quileute Indian] said that Sunday [May 19th] Reagan had stopped the preparations for Dan White's "pot-latch;" that the Indians should remove him. He is always making the Indians trouble. "Reagan," he continued, "had told the Indians that he would recommend a celebration like the one they had last year, but that no "potlatch" would be allowed. The Indians should remove him so that they could get their old ways" (Woodruff 1907).

The restrictions on potlatching must have subsided by 1915,[6] as Fannie Taylor writes in her diary on January 1, 1915; "those that went to Taholah had a big time, a big Potlatch, so Joe [Pullen] said. Jack Hudson not to be outdone is also buying for a feast."

Although the Indian Agency teacher, Albert Reagan, was viewed as a hindrance to traditional ways, he was helpful to those who sought the new ways, such as acquiring land. On November 13, 1907, Reagan wrote Superintendent Woods:

> Charlie Howeattle filed on a claim in 1900 — the filing was rejected, later Charlie was advised by the land office to file again. This Charlie failed to do but has lived on and farmed a part of the tract since 1900 — Recently a Mr. Porter filed on the land for a timber claim. I examined the land Monday and caused Charlie to enter contest before Com. Erickson[7] that the land is better for farming than for timber... (Reagan 1907a).

Albert Reagan and Fannie Taylor were friends. They were both born in Iowa, so perhaps they knew each other before coming to LaPush. Reagan worked for the Indian Service and came to LaPush on July 1, 1905, from Lummi Day School in Bellingham and left on October 15, 1909, for Nett Lake, Minnesota. The Taylor's arrived a year before the Reagan's left, and Fannie and the Reagan's continued to correspond.

Mrs. Albert Reagan and her sister on a snow shoe trip at Nett Lake

Fannie worked for the Indian Service as a teacher at LaPush for six months in 1919 and for ten months between 1922 and 1923. Fannie's government personnel files from the Office of Personnel Management show she was at the Salt River Agency at Scottsdale, Arizona seeking a teaching position in December of 1923. Soon after this she was staying at Cornfields, Arizona where Reagan taught and his wife, Otilla, was a housekeeper at the Indian Day School. In 1924 Fannie worked as a temporary teacher at Fort Defiance Agency, Arizona. After November of 1925, there is no further correspondence in her personnel file, but a Post Office Department letter states she was employed at Fort Defiance from 1924 until 1928. Fannie's personnel file shows that she was beyond the age limit for entrance into the Civil Service, and could

Albert Reagan

W.F. Taylor Surveying

only hold temporary positions. She was 51 in January of 1924. In March of 1928 Reagan transferred to Queets. It is possible that Fannie returned to Mora in 1928, although records indicate she did not officially return to the Mora postmaster position until 1937 when Tealie resigned the post.

Fannie's husband, William. F. Taylor was most likely surveying for the Union Pacific Railroad at the time they moved to Mora and may also have been working for Theodore Rixon on the Olympic Highway in 1909.[8]

After Fannie and W.F. Taylor took over the Mora operations, the following excerpts were recorded in the September, 1909 issue of the Quileute Independent:

- Some days ago the gasoline boat was anchored near James Island, that boat brought much stuff for Mr. Taylor's store, many of the people were working at that time.

- This morning I saw John Bright and his wife [Nina] going up to Mora taking a big load of supplies for Mr. Taylor. Harold Johnson and wife [*Thla-ta-bouth*] are going up to Mora also to take some foods up there for Mr. Taylor.

- Yesterday morning Carl [Black] and Sallie [Black *(Klook-ka-uc)*] went up to Mora on business. They came back in the evening.

- Last Friday Mrs. Taylor and daughter came down visiting Mrs. Reagan.

Although Fannie came to Mora in 1908, her extant journals do not begin until 1914 and continue regularly only through 1915, with sporadic entries in 1916, 1918 and 1922. These entries have been transcribed verbatim and the original diaries are archived in the Olympic National Park collections. Featured here are the diary entries of 1914 and 1915, with a few omissions. The transcriptions have not been changed, except for some minor punctuation, and the addition of Quileute names and first names when found, as well as other relevant details inside brackets. The Quileute words are set in italics. To provide a visual perspective to Fannie's words, many of her wonderful photographs are included and identified whenever possible. A few details from her 1914 diary are supplemented by her daughter Tealie's journal from that same year.

There are a few journal entries that mention sending Indian baskets to various individuals. Often these individuals were museum curators, so the basketry may still be found in these repositories. Anthropologist, Leo Frachtenberg was at LaPush in 1916, and Smithsonian records show he received mail and purchased supplies at Mora while sending ethnological specimens back to George Heye, so it is likely that Fannie had obtained museum contacts from Frachtenberg. In June of 1917, Fannie donated 63 baskets — two representing each style — to the Smithsonian, as well as rattles, horn spoons, fish hooks, a clamshell chisel, a shell and bead necklace, and a Tlokwali house post representing the spirit guardian of the home owner. The Smithsonian holds this collection today.

Fannie's photographs include numerous photos of Quileute

Fannie's shadow

people. Unfortunately, like all of her photos, they are not identified. Even so, they provide an incredible visual history.

Photographs of Fannie are uncertain, but based on several factors, including a photo of Fannie in her late years; we have attempted to find Fannie Taylor among her photographs. Here are a few of those photos:

Fannie circa 1915

Fannie circa 1945

Fannie and Tealie circa 1918

Probably Fannie and Mrs. Reagan at Fort Defiance Indian Agency school

CHAPTER 1

DATEBOOK FOR 1914

Tealie and Lloyd, Mora home and store

1914 THURSDAY 1, JAN.

Began the New Year by making preparations for New Year's dinner. Had two turkey, both young, one weighing 6½# and one 8#. Mr. And Mrs. Keene, [the Superintendent of the school at LaPush] and children, Mr. and Mrs. [Walt and Myrtle] Ferguson,[9] Mr. Womer and son took dinner with us. Mr. F. said his first turkey dinner in Quillayute country, and he has been here over 20 years. Hard rain and wind in p.m.[10] Arnold stayed over night, going out on stage. Eb and Gretta [Morse] were down to the cannery for dinner. Cleve Maxfield with mail, which was not late for a wonder. Beth gave me a lovely burnt wood calendar for New Years. Mary gave me skirt holder and glove case. [Beth and Mary were the daughters of Wesley Smith and Gertrude Bright. In 1914 Beth was 24 and Mary 17 — their farm was about a mile up the road from Mora. Mary was nicknamed Happy by her brother Edward.]

Jan. Friday 2, 1914

Wind blew something fierce the latter part of last night; has continued to blow all day. The surf has thundered all day. Telephone wire is down between here and Quillayute [Prairie], also towards LaPush. Trees have been falling all day.

Made out P.O. reports. Frank and Lucille [Morse] came up after the mail. [Frank and Lucille are the daughters of Samuel Gay (S.G.) Morse and his wife Susan Draper Morse. S.G. purchased the Kinney cannery on the Dickey River on February 13, 1912. There were six Morse children — two sons; Eb (1887) and Hugh (1892); and four daughters, Fanny or Fan (1890), Nell (1895), Frances or Frank (1899), and Lucille (1900), also referred to by Fannie and Tealie as Cile or Tule.]

Morse family - S.G., Susan Draper Morse, Lucille, Nell, Hugh, and Eb

Tealie went back home with them to stay the day. Fanny [Morse] phoned asking for her to stay all night. Suppose the girls are having a fine time to-night. Must write several letters yet. Have lost Moran's[11] letter and do not know where to send [Indian] baskets.

[Tealie (age 17) writes of the same day's events:]

> I went down to see Frank and Cile today. They are such jolly girls, I just love to go down to their place and spend the day. Frank is one of the nicest girls I ever knew. We had a delightful time all day. Frank was making a dress, and it is just as cute as can be. I helped her with it for a while. We had quite a time when we went to bed. We played just like a lot of little kids till about eleven o'clock.

Slough and Morse cannery

1914 SATURDAY 3, JAN.

Frank and Lucille came home with Tealie and spent the day. Gave Lucille Tealie's red cashmere dress and silk skirt. The girls stayed to dinner. I went down to the slough where they left their boat.

Telephone man came in about dark, reported two logs across the road about half way to the [Mora] schoolhouse. Charley [Hagadorn, the mail carrier,] had to leave his rig and bring the mail down on a horse. Received a post card from Lloyd [Taylor,] expect he was in Clallam last night, scow was there. Wind blowing hard again tonight, rained all day.

JAN. SUNDAY 4, 1914

Got up to find the river the highest of the winter and still rising. Rose about four feet during the day. Started to drop about seven p.m., but did not drop far. A large amount of drift has been going down all day. Charley went up and sawed the two logs out, but did not bring down the rig. Not any one up from the cannery. Water up to the timbers under the butcher room. River breaking through by schoolhouse at LaPush. Not many Indians up today. Telephone line down in almost every direction. Wind rising.

Lloyd Taylor, Fannie's son

Cannery with Quillayute River on left, Dickey River on right

JAN. TUESDAY 6, 1914

River two feet higher than Sunday. Grant [Eastman] brought Frank [Morse] up, Frank and Tealie went to Eb's [Morse]. Frank goes out [to high school in Port Angeles] in the morning. One bent of Calawah Bridge went out. Harvey's[12] [Smith] sheep reported drowned. Dock gone at the cannery. [Roy] Jordan came, reported three trees down between Forks and Prairie. Harry Maxfield[13] with mail said he sawed log out. Jack left box of fish to go to Todd for Morse. Sent in M.O. [Mail Order] funds and postal funds.

[Tealie writes:]

> The weather has cleared up today. It seems too good to see a little sunshine and moonlight again. Mamma and I went for a walk this evening. It was real nice.

JAN. THURSDAY 8, 1914

Looks like better weather, river dropping some. High water took out some of wire fence across river. Harvey [Smith] came down, found all his sheep drowned.

JAN. SATURDAY 10, 1914

Began to rain about 10 o'clock last night, been at it all day and still blowing and raining tonight. Mrs. [Edythe] Keene telephoned that [their son] Kenneth had pulled plug from washing machine and scalded himself from his knee down, all the skin coming off. Good thing Dr. Woods [the Indian Agent and Doctor at Neah Bay,] is on the stage coming in today. Asked S.G. [Morse] and family up for Sunday dinner. See Charley Palmer in with freight team for fish.[14] Mary Smith and Lucille Morse here for supper on their way down home for Sunday. Not much mail. Heavy wind and rain. Charley said Floyd[15] [Johnson] was in Clallam with scow Rhoda on Thursday — [telephone] line down.

1914 SUNDAY 11, JAN.

Heavy wind up. Morse had hard time coming up from cannery with four in the boat. Mary [Smith] stayed for turkey dinner. Had a very pleasant visit

School building with support beams after the storm

with Mrs. [Susan] Morse. Dr. Woods came up about 7:30 p.m. Gave Dr. picture I took of Quileute Day School, said it would be of great assistance to him in securing a new school house at LaPush. [The schoolhouse was extremely damaged in the storm on November 26, 1913.]

1914 TUESDAY 13, JAN.

A nice day, sunshine, just as clear as can be. Had to get three meals today [for guests]. Mr. and Mrs. [Henry and Ida] Marshall down; the first time she has been here since Henry went to work up at Beaver on the Alston Fairservice contract [running the stage that carries the mail from Clallam Bay]. Cleve Maxfield telephoned that Jim Clark [county commissioner] and Mr. K.O. Erickson would be down for supper and to stay all night. Do not know where Jim went, K.O. went to Smiths. Received post cards form [Seattle photographic developer] P. Wischmeyer. Sent ones ordered to Dr. Woods [at Neah Bay]. Received a post card from Mrs. [Arilla] Johnson, dated at Sturges, [SD] she says she is soon coming home. Today is my birthday [born in 1873]. Everyone forgot it but myself.

JAN. WEDNESDAY 14, 1914

Began to rain during the night. Will [W.F.] and Hal [George] gone to the ranche. About 12 o'clock last night when making up mail heard telephone ringing, went to phone and found Mr. [Fred] Keene trying to get Forks for to call Dr. [Carl] Koenig. Could not get thru or anyone else on the line. Kenneth [Keene] had quite a severe chill, with heart acting badly. After they got a fire and warmed some milk for him he went to sleep. Lots of good the phone does in case of need.

JAN. SUNDAY 18, 1914

Cold and cloudy, heavy showers. Billy [Hudson] here before I was up, after Doctor. Jim Kay down from Forks on way to Newberts. [Walter Edward Newbert, Theodore F. Rixon, and [James] J.B. Dodge, while surveying for the Union Pacific railroad, filed homesteads from Teahwhit Head to Taylor Point. The Taylor's, acquired the Dodge homestead in 1909.]

Hal George[16]

Tealie came down home, wet to the skin. Had to put Buster in barn, seems afraid of horses. Mrs. Morse asked me down to dinner, but I could not get away. Frank Thompson and another fellow went down to the cannery this evening about dark. Another rainy and windy night; seems to have got the habit.

1914 MONDAY 19 JAN.

Clear and cold. Jerry [Jones] up after a load for Carl [Black]. Mrs. Keene says Dr. is busy tearing down old school house, 20 men at work. Beth [Smith] and Mary [Smith] down, cut out Mary's brown dress, it is going to look fine on her. Wonder what Beth will say when she sees how narrow it is.

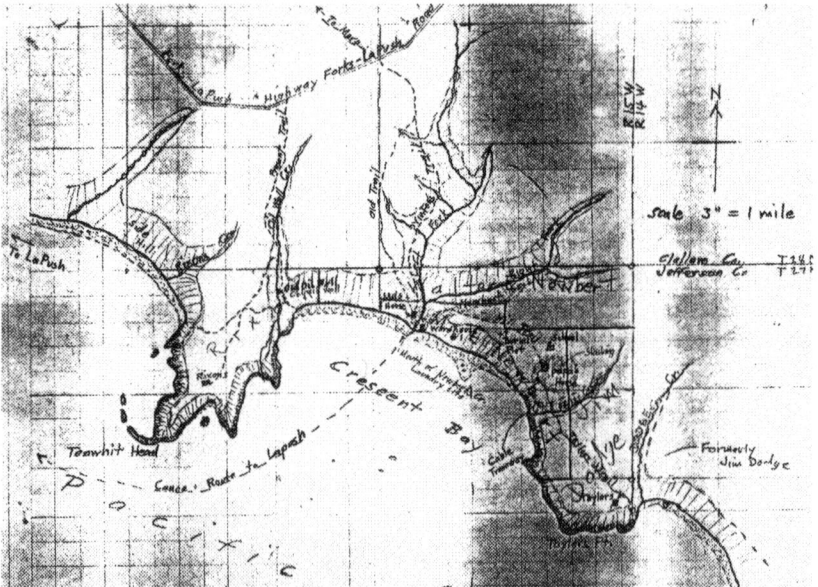

Map of Teawhit Head and Taylor Point

It will be in style at least. Began to rain about two o'clock and finished up the day raining.

JAN. TUESDAY 20, 1914

Another good morning. Put collar on Mackinaw. Swept upstairs and down. Eb went down after [his wife] Gretta and [their son] George. Caught Waddles for Eb to take home with three other ducks. Went home with Eb and Gretta. Came home with Harry Maxfield[17] on the mail wagon. Found Dr. Woods here on his way home. Wesley Smith here with two hogs to go out on the mail. Ten o'clock when mail arrived. Log still in road, Wesley broke both single trees because of it.

1914 WEDNESDAY 21 JAN.

Raining. Had to set alarm and call Dr. Finished Tealie's waist and my Mackinaw. [Art] Wentworth[18] down. Tealie's sweater and fur came last night. Very quiet today. The schoolhouse at LaPush all down and Dr. out to get more lumber to build new school building. Rain still quietly falling. Have not had any wind for several days, but the rain is very persistent.

The day is cold and dark and dreary,
It rains and the wind is never weary.

"Ready for a walk on a rainy day" — unidentified people.

Jan. Thursday 22, 1914

Clear and cold. Dug some parsnips and sent them up to Gretta by Tealie. Mr. Marshall down. Sammy [S.G. Morse] here. Went across the river and fed cattle. Babe looks pretty thin. Beth, Lucille, and Miss [Ruth] Larsen [school teacher at Mora] down for mail. Lucille will be rather lonely without Mary. Mary, Miss Harris and Wesley [Smith] went as far as the prairie tonight; they expect to make tomorrow night's boat. Has been showering lazily tonight in spite of the cold. Got some good oranges from Forks tonight.

1914 Friday 23 Jan.

Clear and cold. Some of the [Quileute] Indians here on their way up the river to fish.

Quileute boys with fish

Jan. Saturday 24, 1914

Snowing, about 1 inch though turned to rain shortly after one o'clock. Baked and made pies. W.F. came home. Phone so cannot ring anymore, broken from generator. P.C. [post card] from Floyd and also from Iva [Hosack]. Her and Ruby are at Neah Bay. Hugh [Morse] and Marjorie [Griffith] married on Sat. last. Charley on mail wagon on time. Began reading "Joyce of the North Woods," think I will like it very much.

1914 TUESDAY 27 JAN.

Ground covered with snow. Snowing heavily. Telephone on the bum. Stormed hard all day. Mail not in till eleven o'clock. Went down after fish broke wheel all to snarl at foot of the hill. Four sacks mail. Received post card album from Mrs. Johnson, box of writing paper from Cleve and Gerty [Maxfield], and chiffon scarf from Mr. Johnson. Mrs. Johnson sent Tealie a cameo ring, which she had brought from Sturges S. Dak. Julia Lee [Chitcha] gave me a very nice basket.

JAN. WEDNESDAY 28, 1914

Still snowing but still not deep on the ground. Tealie went up to [Mora] school. Snow turned to rain about noon. Had to set sheep's leg again. Put splints over knee to keep from slipping down. Sorted out post cards and put some in album. Wind raising when went to bed. Began reading Victor Hugo's "By the order of the King." Joe Marsh down. [Joe Marsh, as superintendent of roads, had four men build the road from Mora to Rialto. He also purchased property at Rialto in 1920, anticipating tourism in the area.]

JAN. FRIDAY 30, 1914

Raining. Sammy Morse up for mail. Dave [Hudson *(Wou a doc ud)*] up, told about storm taking roof off smokehouse, destroying all his vegetables and hay. Carried roof over two-story house back into yard about 50 feet. Tealie finished skirt of black silk dress. [Roy] Jordan came down and fixed telephone — can ring the neighbors now. Still raining tonight.

1914 SATURDAY 31 JAN.

Looks like better weather. Swept upstairs. Got some [Indian] baskets ready to send to [Aunt] Hattie [Hildebrand]. Jordon went to LaPush. Charley said Lloyd and Floyd were at Clallam with *Rhody*. Carl up with list of groceries wanted on the schooner. Lucille went to Eb's last night to stay till Monday, Gretta came home. Charley with mail. Getting colder.

FEB. SUNDAY 1, 1914

Pretty cold during latter part of night. Clear this morning. Going to hurry up work and go to LaPush this p.m. Mr. [Henry] Marshall, [and kids] Helen, and Edwin down. Mr. K[eene] up. Went down to beach with him. After dinner all of us went out around [river] jam. Mr. Keene and children only part way. Kenneth's burnt leg getting well fast; just two small places not healed. Charley says Sven [Sverne] Johnson drove Kit till she dropped dead. [Lloyd] Curtis here when we came home from LaPush. Sally Black not feeling very well.

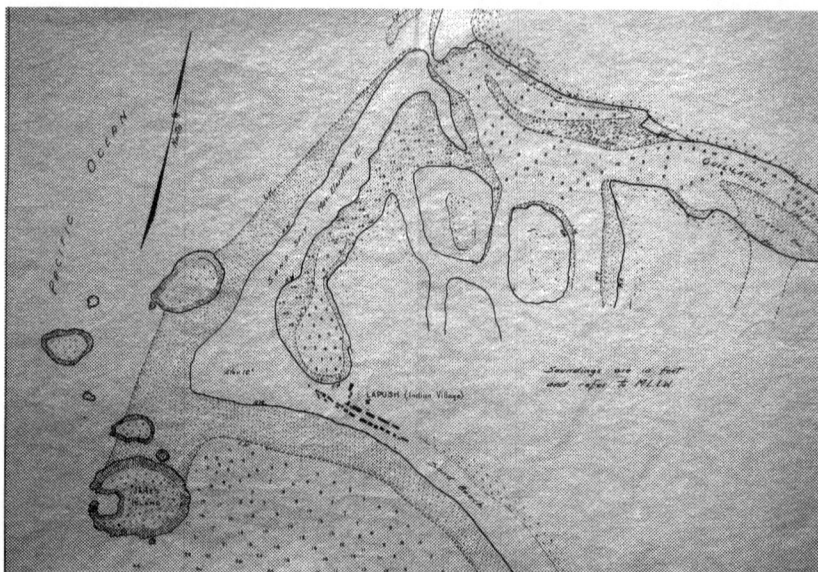

Chart of the mouth of the Quillayute River in 1897

1914 MONDAY 2 FEB.

Clear and ground frozen hard enough to hold a horse. W.F. left for up Sound and Portland, going to stop at Townsend to [Jefferson County] commissioners meeting. Mr. and Mrs. [Fred and Augusta] Christensen down, Mrs. C. for first time. Like her very much. Had chicken dinner and gave the dogs a good feed. Mrs. Ferguson tells me that fish wheel was blown on rock during storm on Thursday last. Still clear and cold.

1914 WEDNESDAY 4 FEB.

Clear and cold. Tealie and I finally got the engine going. Did a lot of washing. Engine stopped about 5 o'clock, carburetor flooded. Eb came down for some things in the evening, says Gretta is feeling better. Left clothes on the line as the moon is shining and sky is clear. Going to be pretty cold tonight. Looked at sheep's leg. Splints are holding break but pressing on foot pretty bad.

FEB. SATURDAY 7, 1914

Looks like better weather. Did lots of work today without accomplishing much. Harry California shooting at three of the boys who were going down the river. Mrs. Yakalader [Jennie Obi, (Wha-los-tub), who was married to Yakalada Obi] here with clams. Took some up to Eb [Morse] and [Art] Wentworth came down there and got part. Ruth, Betty Alexander [Sister of Harvey Smith's wife Adeline], and Otto [Siegfried] here for mail. Charley went up home with them.

Quileute man and possibly Susan Morse

1914 TUESDAY 10 FEB.

Raining. Did not get up till later. Conrad [Williams] here on way up river, says Charlie Howeattle caught 20 fish last night. Fitted the waist of Tealie's black dress. Sammy says Hugh and Marjorie [Morse] are on the stage coming. Eb is going to the fork of the road to meet them. Mr. Keene and the Indians up for mail. Got a calendar from [Mrs. Morganthaler] Washing. Still raining. Blackie had twin lambs. Mailed order to Somers at St. Paul. Paid bills. Mr. K. played guitar.

FEB. FRIDAY 13, 1914

Some rain and fog. Tried to bake a cake, made two and neither one fit to use. Beth [Smith] going to give Tealie some cake. Mr. Morse up. Hugh and Gretta went down to the cannery. Pressed Lucille's dress and fixed collar of green slip. Charley came and got rig. Tealie went too. Beth was to meet them at the schoolhouse. Ruth and Melbourne[19] are going horseback. Would like to see Lucille when she puts on her dress. Maybe Nell will be over.

1914 SATURDAY 14 FEB.

Clear and cold. Kitchen looked so fierce that I had Susie[20] come up and clean things up. Blackie's two-year-old lamb had twins. Susie and I had to throw her and let one suck. Put them in shed in yard. Betty [Alexander] came down to spend Sunday with Tealie. Everyone tired. Charley went up to Wesley's with Beth and Lucille. Lucille pleased with her dress, it fit all right. Received Roosevelt's Autobiography.

Feb. Sunday 15, 1914

A lovely day. Betty and Tealie went to LaPush, say they had a fine time [riding Merry-go-round with Hal George and Rex Ward].[21] Keene started up with the family in a canoe. Mrs. K and the children started to walk around the first riffle [and] got stuck in quicksand. Mrs. K. went to near her waist. Hugh down to meet them. Stayed home and read all afternoon. Charley mad because fish was hard to get up from fish house. Do not blame him. Colty ran horseshoe nail in the foot up near foot of prairie hill. Betty stayed all night.

1914 Monday 16 Feb.

Clear, clouded up some during day. Gretta here on her way to cannery. Marjorie drove her down. Annie and Max [Klahn] here on way to Rixon's. They have bought place up river from W[illiam] Klahn. Susie [Black] and Bessie [Gray] brought clams, were down beach yesterday but tide did not go out far enough as went today. Paid Max for wood, went up to look at it and could only find 16 ricks [8 cords], will have to ask Max where the rest is. Colty not lame on foot. A little cloudy tonight.

1914 Friday 20 Feb.

Sprinkling when got up but cleared up towards noon. Pumped some [water] by hand, and tackled gas engine, which ran a few more turns than has been. *Rhody* did not come down today. Mr. [Walt] Ferguson down, S.G. went up to Eb's. Tealie went up to school. Lucille and Ruth came down, Betty went on down to cannery. The girls going to beach tomorrow. Clouded up at sunset. Cope [Norvel] up with blueback. Sprinkling at bedtime.

Feb. Saturday 21, 1914

Raining with not much looks of a clear up. Ironed. Made pumpkin pie. Mr. K[eene] up. W.F. fixed barn so sheep can go in feed part. Had quite a time, they all wanted to go eat grass after getting a drink, but it was raining too hard. Sheepa was quite determined. Made quite a number of calendars. Put new ribbon on typewriter and practiced some, also studied some. Received a letter from Gordon [Hobucket], and two boxes correspondence cards. Rained hard today with some wind. Nobody up for mail tonight.

[Gordon Hobucket sent a post card (no date) with a photo of Chemawa Indian Boarding School which read:]

Mrs. W.F. Taylor:

Employees' quarters at the other side. Things are somewhat quiet around here just now. The children are at the hop fields now. Am going out to take the rest of my leave.

Respt. Hobucket

1914 SUNDAY 22 FEB.

Misty this morning but cleared up later. Mr. and Mrs. Marshall down. Tealie, Betty, Lucille, and Ruth went to LaPush. Dutch here for first time in two weeks. Read *Saturday Evening Post*. Keep sheep in yard. Wrote several letters. Sent order for roses to Lilys and also to Good and Reese of Springfield, Ohio. Wrote to Gordon. Betty came back early; the others went on James Island. Charley came down late, kicking about size of fish boxes again; think I would quit. Raining again tonight.

FEB. WEDNESDAY 25, 1914

Clear and quite cold. West Wind but changing to south. Hal [George], Wilson [Payne], Max [Hudson], Dewey P[ullen], Billy [Hudson], Ernest [Obi], Joe [Cole] and Isaac [Lee] here on way to Tulalip [*Tsalilitqw*][22] after lumber. Mr. [Jesse] Maxfield and Poole here. Mr. [Henry] Poole looking much better than in September. Jim [Clark] here last night, left this morning. Fanny [Morse], Marjorie [Griffith], and George and Jean [Morse] went down to cannery for an hour. Gas engine runs better today. Lloyd called up from Clallam. *Rhody* went on up to Neah Bay. Cleaned up magazines. Took some upstairs. Clear tonight!

Quileute woman on James Island (holding Fannie's camera case)

Eb Morse ranch

1914 THURSDAY 26 FEB.

Raining. Got papers ready to send to Fred and Glen Young. Mr. [Albert] Reagan says in letter of Tuesday that school building burnt [at Nett Lake, Minnesota]. Has rained all day. Wind howling about 40 miles. Boys went down river with rafts of lumber. One big raft and three small ones at fish camp had head wind all the rest of the river. Came near drifting out to sea, wind off shore. Canoes could not tow them in. Keene has to wade out and get hold of pole to help hold. Lloyd came in on stage. Cleve [Maxfield] lost on prairie.

FEB. FRIDAY 27, 1914

Clear. Lloyd started engine and I did quite a washing. Engine began to talk. Lloyd took it apart. Mr. and Mrs. Theo Klahn down. Gretta, Hugh, Fanny, and George went down to cannery. Lucille went home. John Smith down for mail. Began "Riders of the Purple Sage" by Zane Gray. A story of Mormonism in 1871. Did not put clothes on line for fear it would rain and blow. Looks like good weather tonight.

MAR. SUNDAY 1, 1914

Clear in spots. Killed turkey, had Charley ask Beth to dinner. Ruth and Mary Hutsell also. Everyone seemed to have a good time. Lucille and Sammy came up. House at cannery afire this a.m. Came near burning down, would but for raining. Beth and I walked down to lower end of island. Tealie went up to stay at Lucille's tonight. Had quite a time getting sheep into the barn. New moon, clear and cold, northwest wind all day today.

1914 MONDAY 2 MAR.

Mist or maybe you would call it rain. W.F. and Lloyd tore down fence around turkey yard. Harvey down with 48 sheep.[23] Hugh [Morse] down home. Old Web Jones[24] up. Went up to Eb's for supper; had a dandy time and a dandy supper. Walked up and back. Came back about ten o'clock. Heard Mrs. [Martha] Mayberry [Maybury] had small pox. Suppose there will be some more cases. Raining but not much wind.

A basket woven mussel shell rattle from the Taylor collection at the Smithsonian, 2005.

MAR. TUESDAY 3, 1914

Clear, looks as if showers might follow through. Picked up clothes that blew down last night. Straightened up papers in P.O. S.G. and George up. Oil well fellow came back from Ferguson's. Charley on mail. Baked bread. Eggs from Earl Wilson's [married to Mary Marsh]. Gyp [the dog] bothering all day. Bought rugs [cedar mats?] and rattles from Susie. Old Powder horn yesterday from old Web Jones, also beaver teeth. Clear tonight with some fog.

1914 WEDNESDAY 4 MAR.

Fairly nice this a.m. Hung up clothes. Engine sure hot while pumping. Lloyd went to beach. Worked in front yard cleaning up grass. Planted hop roots by closet. Washed clothes enough to fill lines again. Took down clothes, which were dry. Lloyd and Will [W.F.] fixing turkey yards. Read Sunday papers. Clear. Carl [Black] reported *Rhody* behind James Island. Rather doubtful. Hal [George] says he saw her too. A stormy looking sunset.

MAR. THURSDAY 5, 1914

Misty. East wind. *Rhody* showed up about 11 a.m. Had come down yesterday but saw it was too rough to come in so went to sea one hour and north an hour for location from [Umatilla] lightship, had only 5 ft tide to come in on. Made it all right but got stuck on riffle this side LaPush, cannot come up till morning. Charley in at 8 o'clock, guess the team must of run away. Beth down for mail, Charley went up with her. Wrote Dr. Woods for Carl [Black]. Got letter from Gordon [Hobucket]. Misty and warmer.

1914 FRIDAY 6 MAR.

Oregon mist all day. *Rhody* tried to get up river but got stuck on upper part of last riffle. Carl took most of his things off. Quileute boys took part of things off in whaleboat. Eb down for load of posts for barn. Lucille went home. Floyd tried to get *Rhody* off on evening tide but is stuck hard yet. Still misting this evening.

Unloading *Rhody* onto scow

MAR. SATURDAY 7, 1914

Cloudy. *Rhody* off bar at high tide. Finished unloading. Indians went to Forks to play basketball. Had toothache all day. Face swelled. Floyd said I had list to port, felt like it. Mrs. [Ida] Marshall here. New sewing machine looks fine. Hope it sews that way. Finished waist, all but buttonholes. Still cloudy but not raining. Sea calm.

1914 SUNDAY 8 MAR.

Clear and nice. *Rhody* went out on morning tide. Tealie and Charley went to Harvey's. Beth and Ruth went up Saturday. Marjorie and Gretta, and [Gretta's daughter] Jean Morse, went to cannery. Walked down to bar with them. Head aching bad when I came back, went to bed after taking bromo-quinine. W.F. and Lloyd put up gas lamp. Got up and helped Lloyd get supper. Made up part of mail. Clear.

1914 TUESDAY 10 MAR.

Clear. Worked some on flower garden. Tealie made skirt; it looks pretty. Gordon [Hobucket] left for home. Banner coughed and stamped around all night. Baked bread. Got some clams from Mrs. [Susie] Tim [mother of

James Island from First Beach. Middle man may be Chris Morganroth II

Daniel White]. Had clam fritters for dinner. [Henry] Nolan and the son of Dr. Douglas came down in a canoe with one of the Indians. Tealie and I walked up the road to meet Charley who was rather late as he broke the ringbolt on his rig just this side of Eb's. Ruth and Lucille down. Both took supper at Hutsell's. A beautiful night.

MAR. WEDNESDAY 11, 1914

Clear, but clouding up. Breakfast on the installment plan. Nolan and Douglas went to LaPush, went to cannery on return and are still there, hope they stay. W.F. went to the ranch. Went up with Eb and Gretta to get some wild strawberry plants. Worked some more in flower garden. Planted lilies, which came last night. Only part of that order arrived. Capt. Saux [*Whahub*] down, has new horse. Looks like rain tonight.

1914 THURSDAY 12 MAR.

Raining. Planted onions in the front yard. Douglas and Nolan went back to Forks. K.O. [Erikson][25] here on way to cannery. Baked bread. Mr. Keene up for mail, which was somewhat late. Roses for myself and Mrs. [Myrtle] Ferguson came on mail.[26] Two numbers of *Delineator*. Dewey Cleveland and Francis Gray went up to Wesley to be married without securing a license. Raining and looks like more of it. Did not get to bed till after 12 o'clock.

MAR. SUNDAY 15, 1914

Looks like more rain. Forks basketball team went to LaPush to play. Harvey [Smith family] went down also. S.G. would not let Lucille go because Lee

"Sea Lion Rocks from south showing sea lions"

[Palmer] was here. W.F. came up from ranche. Began raining about two o'clock. Crowd came back from LaPush. All the folks down here got in and rode up with Ebs. S.G. looked glum because Lee went. Made up M.O. books and sent remittance to Seattle $247.43. Charley good and mad about [Walter] Newbert's mail. Raining hard.

MAR. THURSDAY 19, 1914

Not so fine looking as yesterday. Got breakfast and went to the island for Colty. Snokums did not want to come up. Lloyd made a harrow. Cleaned up things in the office. Began letter to [State Representative (Albert)] Alfred Johnson [1913-1915 2nd District]. Harvey [Smith] and his wife [Adeline] down with sheep, the lambs look fine. Jim Clark and Jim Kay here. Mr. Lamb down to go out on stage. Fanny and I go up to Eb's or got part way rather and came back with Charley.

1914 FRIDAY 20 MAR.

Clear. Jim Clark went to Forks with Theodore Klahn who was down for a load. Baked or Tealie did rather. Indians did not go sealing, west wind.[27] A few went to Sea Lion Rocks. Tealie and I went down to Keene's for the evening, came home about ten. A lovely clear night. Lloyd reading when we came back. Read some of the stories in *Cosmopolitan*.

MAR. SATURDAY 21, 1914

Clear. Theodore Klahn down for load. Jim Clark went up with him. Baked. Quite an excitement caused by operators at Clallam phoning Floyd had passed out of the cape at 5:30 a.m.; when three o'clock came and no boat we were very much worried. Finally [Albert] Johnson telephoned Floyd was at Seattle. Worry all for nothing. Ruth, Mary Hutsell, and Lucille came down from schoolhouse with Lloyd. Ruth stayed all night. Crockery came, three pieces broken. Cloudy and threatening rain.

Shaker meeting

Tealie writes:

> Of course it had to rain today 'cause Ruth and I wanted to go to
> LaPush. We didn't get up till eleven so didn't have much time to go
> anywhere. We wanted to go down to LaPush to a Shaker meeting,
> but it rained so hard we didn't go or rather we couldn't go. It cleared
> up real nice after dark, tho.

1914 TUESDAY 24 MAR.

Fairly clear, but rained by ten, hailed also, kept up at intervals all day. Ironed
some. Jim Kay came back from ranch. Cut out and made a dress for Doris.
Took my sewing and went to cannery. Mrs. M[orse] and Fanny helped with
things for Mrs. Deitlefson. Sammy made a lot of fun of us, said we would
be busy all summer. Fan came up and we finished the things. Cleve on the
mail.[28] Things did not come on mail from Portland. Check returned for
Dr. Wood's signature. Raining. Wilson Payne's lost their baby.

1914 THURSDAY 26 MAR.

Cloudy. Mr. and Mrs. S.G. and Fanny went up to Eb's. Finished ironing.
Made Doris [Keene] another dress. Gretta down on way to S.G's. Stayed
till after mail. W.F came up from ranch bringing strawberry plants and
onions. Received new scales from P.O. department good for 100#. Letter
from Fish Commissioner Darwin requesting citizenship papers [perhaps it
was necessary to have a license to mail seal fur]. Told him they were on file in
his office already. Ruth down for mail, Charley [Palmer] went through it as
usual. Raining but cold, hail showers all day.

MAR. FRIDAY 27, 1914

Clear most of the night, no wind. Wind came up about daylight, clear and cold. NW wind. Tealie went to school, Mrs. Morse, Gretta, and George also. Ruth came down, going home with Lucille. Planted some strawberry plants in the front yard. Put time on garden till my lungs were full and smarting. Lloyd fixed fences and W.F. put wire around desk. Part of order from Western Dry Goods, sheeting not on invoice — thing wanted worst. Clear tonight and still cold. Baked bread.

[Tealie writes:]

> Ruth [Palmer] went down with Cile tonight to stay till Sunday. She will only be here one more Sunday and then she is going east.[29] I wish I was in her place in a way. I would like to take the trip east that she is going to, but can't so I need not talk about it anymore.

1914 SATURDAY 28 MAR.

Cloudy, occasional rain. Went down over island looking for Colty and Snokums when they were back of the barn. Floyd called up from Clallam, said he did not think it possible to bring the *Rhody* in the river. Joe Pullen says it is better now than when Floyd was in last time. Harvey down with some horses to put across the river. Scrubbed. Rained quite a little this afternoon. Butter did not come. Not many [guests] here tonight.

MAR. SUNDAY 29, 1914

Showery, Charley did not go to Smith's last night, was here for breakfast. Mr. Keene was up. Three Dutchmen were down from Quillayute going to the beach. Read some, mostly newspapers. Wentworths [Arthur V. and Maud][30] have another one in the family [Arthur Jr]. Lucille and Ruth went up to A.W. Smith's. Tealie and I went down to Keene's. Took two dresses for Doris, she took quite a fancy to pink sash on the white one. Came home about ten. Clear over land, a big storm over the ocean. Thunder.

1914 WEDNESDAY 1 APRIL

Sun shining. Mrs. S.G. [Morse] went up to see Beth. Made up quarterly and M.O. accounts. Read papers. Jordon went to LaPush to repair Keene's phone. Put it on the bum entirely. Max Klahn down. Went down to [sand] bar with Mrs. Morse when she went home. Almost out of butter, Peterson says he will sure send some next mail. Cloudy.

APRIL SATURDAY 4, 1914

Rain. The *Rhody* came in about 8:30. Came in by the old channel north of the big island, got stuck on the riffle by the old camp. Mr. and Mrs. Keene up, packed the kids in packsacks. Doris thought it was fine, as were also the black bloomers. Lloyd and Eb went to Forks for the basketball game. General Manager of Jefferson Oil Co. at Forks. Floyd said he saw Fred and Hattie [Hildebrand] during Alaska Celebration Parade. Cloudy but not raining. Floyd slept ashore.

1914 SUNDAY 5 APRIL

Clear. Floyd and W.F. went after boat at Morse's. Joe Pullen, Hal [George] and [Harold] Johnson helped unload. [Henry] Marshall, [Fred] Christensen, and Ollie Smith were down for oats. Beth [Smith] and Charley [Palmer] were out on *Rhody*. Beth thinks is all O.K. Hugh and Marjorie went down to the cannery to stay while S.G. went out. Floyd [Johnson] took *Rhody* to cannery to load Captain's [Al Johnson's] stuff, came up and lay here. Lloyd came from Forks. Clear and cold.

Doris Keene with Tealie's Indian Basket on her head. The same basket appears on a wall in a photograph of Tealie with her violin on page 64.

1914 SATURDAY 11 APRIL

Cloudy. Mina Smith[31] and children and Dad [Frank] Marsh down. Mina and children went on to the beach. Jack Hudson here, took horses over for her. Jack just back after absence of four years. Mina came back and went to Wesley's. Indians sealing, all had saltwater in drinking casks. Charley did not go up to Wesley's tonight, already too many there. Mr. Keene up for the mail. Cloudy and some shower. Mrs. S.G. went to Eb's with Lloyd and Tealie.

Mina Smith and children (Dorothy, Alice, Archer, David, and Hazel) on beach at LaPush circa 1911.

Rhododendron leaving cannery

April Sunday 12, 1914

Cloudy. Indians up for mail. Eb, Gretta, George, Jean, and Mrs. S.G. went down [to cannery], asked me to Easter dinner. Had quite a time looking for Snokums, when he had gone to LaPush with Eb's team, [and] came back with them. Marjorie and Lucille came up for me. Harvey's here with cook stove to take to house at LaPush. Mrs. Ferguson sent me Lady Gay rose and tiger lily. Mrs. S.G. gave me dahlia bulb and chrysanthemum. Lloyd and Tealie home from Forks. Raining.

1914 Monday 13 April

Raining. Went back to bed with a headache, did not stay long, got up to get breakfast. Did not do much but read today. Indians had to get up in night and put their launches in the slough to keep the ten-foot tide from taking them to sea. Saturday night tide came near getting Joe's [Pullen] — took it to the edge of the bar. Tealie took buggy back and is staying all night. Lucille is still at George's too. Quite windy all day. Rain also.

April Tuesday 14, 1914

Rain and wind all day. Read the papers and sewed some. Mended shirts. Arthur [*Howeattle*] up about the Web Jones place. Is to send papers up. Charley with mail. Apples and some of the groceries on mail. All but paper bags. Mary [Smith] and her sister came in on stage. Raining.

1914 Wednesday 15, April

Sun shine in spots. W.F. came home after I had gone to Gretta's. Walked up about noon. Gretta insisted on my having lunch, had some dandy cream. William Penn came up [from LaPush] to work for Eb [Morse]. Lucille, George, Jean, and I went to see the trees that were lightning struck, with

George as guide. He took us down the hill beyond the new barn, along the foot of the hill and up the old Ferguson road. A long ways around, he also took a tumble down the hill. Cloudy.

APRIL SATURDAY 18, 1914

Raining. Ironed. Rather a quiet day. Yesterday Lloyd hauled puncheons and W.F. put them down on trail by warehouse. Will not be so muddy for Colty next time they unload the boat. S.G. came home. Eb went to fork of road to meet him and brought him down. 8 o'clock and no mail yet. Charley should be on time though as it is Saturday and he would be able to go to Smith's. Raining.

APRIL MONDAY 20, 1914

Clear. An unusually nice day. Tealie went to cannery and the whole family went up to the [river] jam. Tealie found mast support and paddle with Lloyd's name on it that had lain in the jam 4½ years. Colty ran away and came home. W.F. followed her until he found the picket rope. She plunged into the river when he arrived. Snokums jumped the fence, got one hind foot caught in top wires, and did not hurt him any. Clear and cold. Set out cabbages.

1914 TUESDAY 21, APRIL

Clear and cold. Weeded hot bed and looked for hen's nests. Tealie cut blue serge skirt. I made serge bloomers for Lloyd and then he decided to not play ball, so, I get the bloomers. Marjorie and Hugh up for mail. Frank Batalph on mail. Dr. Woods and Jim [Clark] came in, stayed all night. All but Dr. and myself stayed up till daylight playing cards. Only way to have [mail] carrier up in the a.m. Clear and cold.

APRIL WEDNESDAY 22, 1914

Clear. Jim, S.G., and Hugh went up to look over school section [for new school on Quillayute Prairie]. Dr. went to LaPush. Read the papers. Set white hen on duck eggs. Received a letter from Mrs. A[nderson] last night. W.F. called up and wanted some things brought down [to ranch]. Told him I

Rhody, Pearl, and scow offshore from cannery

Ern Fletcher working rope

would come tomorrow. Ern [Fletcher] came in the river this a.m. and came up to Mora this p.m. Ern and Lloyd came in and got some bread then went aboard and had supper. Clear.

1914 THURSDAY 23 APRIL

Cloudy, hailed about 10 a.m. Got pack ready and started for the ranche. Lloyd took Colty and Snokums and Teddy across. Snokums tried to walk on Teddy who got too badly scared to even keep in sight. Went back to the river and had Lloyd call him, but nothing doing. Got to second hill and heard him howling, heard him at intervals all the rest of the way, but he was right at my heels when I arrived at the gate [to the ranche]. Snokums was pretty tired. Cloudy.

APRIL FRIDAY 24, 1914

Cloudy by spells. Did not do much but read. Snokums got bad and had to be shut up in the barn on a short rope. W.F. and I went down the beach nearly to Arthur's [Howeattle] place [at Strawberry Point]. Ocean calm. Ern [Fletcher]

Fannie's dog on beach near Strawberry Point south of ranch

Mouth of Scott Creek, Taylor Point on right, Teahwhit head behind it

went down to [Destruction] Island. Planted dahlia and gladiolus bulbs. W.F. put fence around garden so the horses could go loose. Has fence along top of the hill. Thick [fog], cannot see light at Island, only at intervals.

APRIL SUNDAY 26, 1914

Wind, rain and hail all day, did not pick up much sea though. Spent most of the day writing. Read some. W.F. called[32] up and [was] told Jesse Maxfield was dead,[33] died very suddenly last night. Eb [Morse] came and butchered the calf. Will have some milk now. Raining.

1914 MONDAY 27 APRIL

Clear, but bush pretty wet. Intended to go up [to ranch] by way of Newbert's, but it is too damp. Teddy and I took our time coming up, did not feel very well. The idea is Mr. Maxfield died of ptomaine poison, symptoms were of that anyway [newspaper said it was heart failure (PAOL 1914a)]. Went to bed early as I was tired. Going to bury Mr. M tomorrow. Clear and cold.

APRIL TUESDAY 28, 1914

Clear. Carl [Koenig] telephoned and asked if I wanted to go to the funeral with them. Mr. Morse drove up. Hugh and Marjorie walked. The

Fannie hiking on puncheon trail

Quileute couple with canoe at spring near Mora

Indians stopped at the spring [west of Mora] for lunch. Met the County Commissioners, Joe Marsh, Lloyd Curtis, and Cliff Wilson at the upper end of Eb's place. Mrs. Maxfield and Mrs. Eldridge were down here. Tealie got dinner for them. Mrs. M. was too worn out to go to the grave and Annie[34] had to keep up in front of her mother, so Jimmy sent his mother down. W.F. went to the ranch yesterday. Harvey's folks [A.J. and Mary Smith] went to the beach to camp.

APRIL THURSDAY 30, 1914

Clear. Lloyd and Curtis made up books and made out statements last night. Got Eli's [son of *Sea-it-kus Ward*] horse and took turns riding to fork. Nolan sold piano to Billy Iverson and auctioned off even [George] Jeter's cow and frying pans. Heard [Ern's boat], the *Albatross* was wrecked on Destruction Island last Sat. the a.m. after leaving here. Just saved the engine. Dr. Koenig and Esther McCorkle married. Clear.

MAY SATURDAY 2, 1914

Cloudy. Went to Keene's for the day. Mrs. K. and I made dresses for Doris. Mrs. K. had one awful time with the one she made, had to rip out seams till it was like making two garments. I have the white and one pink dress to take up to finish. Came home to milk. A Mr. Ryan came in on the stage to spend Sunday. Guess he was looking for school marms. Raining.

MAY MONDAY 4, 1914

Clear. Tealie and I went to Earl Wilson's [on Bogachiel River], going up to Earl's road [got a ride] with Eb. Eb was down for three shovels, had driven with Gretta from there to Joe's [Marsh] for a bed and dishes, stopped at [Dan] Shearer's tent and got roll of canvas; at the bridge found it was Shearer's clothing instead of tent. Had to go down the trail to opposite Earl's house to get across. Was hungry enough to eat one of the dogs. Mary [Marsh-Wilson] had lots to eat; told her it was a good thing. Clear and cool.

1914 TUESDAY 5, MAY

Clear. Had breakfast at 7:30, early for us. Helped Mary on the work. Carl, Walter [Mary and Earl's son] and I went to the long meadow to take pictures; when we came back found Mary and Tealie had taken Clifford [Mary and Earl's other son] and gone up to Cliff's [Earl's brother]. Walter and I went too, took pictures down by the river of Chimacum [horse] and Walter, also of Mary and the rest of the bunch. In the afternoon Walter and I went up to Cliff's again. The baby has a badly burned hand. See Cliff felled a tree on the barn. Unusually warm and clear.

Cliff Wilson's children (note the baby's bandaged hand)

"John Leyendecker" farm

MAY WEDNESDAY 6, 1914

Clear with promise of another warm day. Walked up to Lyendecker's road, and rode down from there with Eddie [Leyendecker]. Took pictures at Lyendecker's.

Eddie brought us across the river. Stopped at [Walter and Myrtle] Ferguson's [overlooking the Quillayute River] a few minutes. Mr. F. getting ready to shear sheep. Walt here when we got home. Eb butchering muttons. Ed Smith's just planting potatoes. Mary said they had been working hard. Erdest waved good bye till as long as we could hear him.

1914 THURSDAY 7, MAY

Cloudy, misty all day. We did not come home any too soon. If there were any clean dishes they were hid. Dry goods came while we were away; the serge is fine. Charley with the mail. S.G., Hugh, and Nell went to Eb's. Babe had a calf yesterday and this a.m. I had a time milking her. Will have a good piece of meat and lots of milk soon. Tealie put Buster's wool to soak with Ivory soap. Raining, but looks like clearing up.

MAY FRIDAY 8, 1914

Cloudy. Baked bread. Lloyd cleaned the tank. Engine does not work on new spark plugs. W.F. and Lloyd fixed fence on the island to keep sheep from pasture. Harvey went home. Tenas Betty[35] did not want to go, likes LaPush better. Harvey took some sheep up for butchering. Tealie's ankle does not bother her so much now. Mrs. Morse gave me some plants, some rooted. Clear.

1914 SATURDAY 9, MAY

Clear. My knee got hurt slightly this a.m. when I went to milk. Suppose it will be sore now. S.G. went to Forks. [Lloyd] Curtis asked Tealie to go to the dance and then fooled her by not coming after her. Charley rather sore about

Boy with Calf

it. Starbuck and three fellows going up the beach, on the stage. Two other prospectors and a picture man also. Did not know they were coming till the stage was at Maxfield's.[36] Lloyd went to Forks, rode Colty. Clear

MAY SUNDAY 10, 1914

Clear. Got up early to get breakfast for men to get out to sea. Jack Ward took Starbuck's crowd to the mine in a canoe. Things rather quiet. Mr. and Mrs. Keene and babies up for dinner and spent the day. Doris had a big time. Wanted to eat the dog feed and drink coal oil. Floyd [Johnson] was at Clallam Bay on his way to Neah Bay. Some one done a lot of calling on the phone after we went to bed but I could not get up. Charley got a case of milk from Carl.

1914 MONDAY 11 MAY

Clear. Lloyd home about 11 a.m. Foggy on the ocean with a heavy west wind. Some more of the Indians went up to the road camp to work. Most of them are pretty hard up. Put two grips [holding devices] with fish outside, they smelt too loud. Knee getting so sore I can hardly use it, but there is so much to do. Bought a dried Pelican skin with pitch from old Webberhard (my maunna)[37] [sic]. Floyd did not come down today [with the *Rhody*]. Clear. Morton Penn cut down tree for wood.

Pelican skin on right in first photo by Fannie and at the Smithsonian in 2005.
Pelican gullet has pitch block inside.

In June of 1917 Fannie donated the following to the Smithsonian
National Museum, the pelican skin must be in "other" category.

2   ceremonial rattles used during the Tsa'yeq ceremonial

2   ceremonial rattles used during the Tlkkwali ceremonial

1   ceremonial rattle used during the whaling ceremonial

3   hooks for catching codfish

1   salmon club

1   cedar box

63   baskets, two specimens of each type of basketry made by
     Quileute women

19   other items including 6 rattles, 3 horn spoons, 4 hooks, clam-
     shell chisel, hammer, shell and bead necklace.

MAY TUESDAY 12, 1914

Clear. The *Rhody* down at noon but had to wait till three o'clock to get in.
Got stuck on the bar by the jam, not enough water. [Adam] Copeland and
Whitcomb here for a load and Jake Hawn [Hahn] in his auto with Lovegren,
who was in to inspect no. 6 Jefferson [oil well]. Had a houseful. Lloyd and
Floyd staid up till two o'clock to bring the *Rhody* up the river. Not much mail
for Tuesday. Whitcomb went to Klahns. Wentworth down. [His wife] Maud
still poorly. Harvey down with rest of wool. Clear.

1914 WEDNESDAY 13, MAY

Clear. Jakie [Hahn] and Lovegren went right after breakfast. Joe Pullen,
Johnson Black, and Walter Jackson helped unload. Jerry [Moriarity] came for
Carl's goods. Copeland went at noon with load. Sherman [Parker] down for
Jim's seed oats. All through unloading early. The boys pretty tired. Went to

Oil tower at J.O.F. Anderson's ranch below Fern Hill - Grace (Anderson) Fraker peeking out the door

bed early. Knee giving a lot of trouble. Floyd not sure about going out in the a.m. Clear. Turkey setting on stump by apple tree came off with 10 turkeys.

MAY THURSDAY 14, 1914

Clear. Did not know Floyd was here till away after breakfast. He did not feel well. Will wait till tomorrow morning and take order with him. Went to the mouth of the river and back on the *Rhody*. Starbuck and Stewart back [from mine] to go out in the a.m. Tealie going up to stay a few days with Mrs. Sult, as Mr. Sult, Eb, Hugh and Nell went out to Angeles yesterday. Have more than a load for the *Rhody* now. Cleve [Maxfield] on the mail. Clear. Henry Marshall down. Turkeys hatched 10 poults.

MAY SATURDAY 16, 1914

Clear. W.F. went to the ranche. Took Colty then turned her loose to come home. Lloyd went to Forks. My knee pretty lame, making it hard to do the work. Not any letter mail, put off at Gettysburg [about 18 miles west of Port Angeles] by mistake. Hugh came home. S.G. up to meet him. Charley shaved before going to bed. Roy Jordan here [from Sappho]. Two men that went up the beach, Warrick and partner came in from Sandy Point, put up tent and going to camp till Monday stage. [Tealie's diary says Mr. Kelly came down from the Gold Mine on the 17th.] Roy [Jordon] had supper at the cannery. Clear and cool.

1914 SUNDAY 17, MAY

Clear. Jordon left right after breakfast. Not many here, things very quiet. Gretta came and her and I went to the cannery for dinner. Mrs. Morse had great time burning her dinner. Lucille and Jean went to Sunday school and afterwards to Edward's [Smith]. Peterson, former editor of the *Clallam Bay Record*, came in from Dickey Lake, going out on the a.m. stage. Mr. [T.F.] Rixon here while I was away. Wrote to Mrs. [Caroline] Rixon.

Caroline Rixon on right with Beardsley trout

MAY MONDAY 18, 1914

Clear. Tealie came home, as did Lloyd. Came near breaking my knee yesterday, just succeeded in resetting the cap. Today it is somewhat stiff but that is all. Made one apron and read some. Marjorie [Griffith Morse] has a lovely aluminum kettle as fine as I ever saw. Hugh brought her a set of silver knives and fork, community wear; initialed.[38]

Nice and clear, should of washed as everything is dirty. [Charles] Hosack here. Came up the beach. Says Ern is going to get an automobile.

1914 TUESDAY 19, MAY

Clear. Made three aprons. Must make some work dresses. Mrs. David Hudson [Ella] brought me a fine big basket, Potlatch [Chinook Jargon word meaning "a gift" or "to give"]. David got some supplies and went to Rixon's [ranch at Teahwhit Head]. Made punch. Tealie and I walked up to Gretta's and came back with the mail. Eb, Nell, and George on the stage. Nell came on home. Harvey put Topsy and the colts across the river, Mrs. H[arvey Smith] sent down a dozen eggs by the mail. Basketball came; the girls can have a good time. Frank Batalph on the mail. Old [knee] cap awful lame. Clear. Lloyd plowed across the river.

Teahwhit Head

MAY WEDNESDAY 20, 1914

Clear. Got up at daylight and called Frank [Batalph], did not do much good to have him sleep in the house. Turkeys alright. Hosack back, supposed he was in Moclips by now. The *Skagit* up, poked a hole in her on a snag in the river. She lay on the riffle all day. Tealie cut out cream colored dress. Tealie and I worked in the garden. Lloyd planted oats and harrowed. Eb down, wanted picture of Tealie working in the garden. Big fire up the Solduck,[39] heavy smoke, warm and clear.

1914 THURSDAY 21, MAY

Warm, smoky, but not much wind. Had the engine running to wash. Wish we had hose for the garden, everything is so dry. Tealie finished cream colored skirt and made waist, all but the neck trimming. Clothes got dry. Charley on the mail. Frank [Batalph] quit and gone on the Hoh with Curtis. Finished letter to Mr. Reagan. Picked wool. Intend to make some comforters this summer. Will get Harvey to shear the lambs, and keep their wool. Farwell on stage. [Raymond Farwell was the first school teacher for District 36 — Newbert, Taylor, and Rixon children. The schoolhouse was on the Newbert property- see map, page 6].

MAY FRIDAY 22, 1914

Friday. Very warm. Washed, the clothes would dry as fast as you could put them on the line. In the afternoon heavy smoke from the NE showing fire was getting into the green timber. Wind pretty heavy. Burnt ferns fell here. The fire must be pretty bad from the looks of things here. Farwell came on last night's mail, went on down to Keene's. Lloyd got hose and dampened the roof. Was almost afraid to light fire in stove, things were so dry.

Neah Bay dock

1914 SATURDAY 23, MAY

Hot as all get out. Floyd in Clallam last night, said he would be down today. The wind has been pretty strong and the sea is getting rough. Ern down with new automobile, which he bought at Aberdeen and drove to Seattle. Miss Cox and Mr. Williams with him, they staid overnight. Clear and warm. Ern rather stingy with his car, never offered us a ride.

MAY SUNDAY 24, 1914

Cloudy. Got early breakfast so the folks could go to Forks. Tealie went to the cannery. Mrs. K[eene] had on her new plaid coat, I told her it could be heard a mile. Began raining about eleven. Rained pretty hard all afternoon. *Rhody* at Neah Bay. Read up for a weeks papers.

1914 MONDAY 25, MAY

Raining and some wind but not much sea. Tealie getting wool ready for Floyd's mattress. Cliff [Wilson] has been doing a lot of work this year; the road will have gravel from Clallam Bay to Mora. Two pits will be opened on Quillayute Prairie, one at the Sippy place and one on the lower end of the prairie. Art Wentworth is sorry he did not take my bet. S.G. went to Angeles.

MAY TUESDAY 26, 1914

Cloudy, light SW wind. Floyd wired asking about the ocean. Answered ocean calm, wind SW 20 miles an hour. Dr. has trouble to get his lumber down. When the ocean is good the *Tatoosh* cannot come. It is not so easy to get a scow around, even in the summertime. Tealie's plaid coat came and you can hear her as you can Mrs. Keene. Showery.

1914 WEDNESDAY 27, MAY

Clear but some wind. Floyd still at Neah Bay. The girls are having a great time learning to skate. They are covered with black and blue places, but are still courageous. I wonder how long I could stand up, as it has been many years since I had skates on. The girls wear their bloomers all the time when skating.

MAY THURSDAY 28, 1914

Partly clear. Nell and Lucille here. Tealie went down to roller skate. The girls are mostly bumps nowadays; the skates are too much for them. Cut stakes for peas. Nell got her boots full of water. The pears look like they had been refrosted. The white worms are bothering some. Made a cake. For a wonder it was good. Baked bread. Was pretty warm today.

Nell and Tealie in bloomers

MAY SATURDAY 30, 1914

Clear. The boys [Lloyd and Floyd] went down early this a.m. after the boat and got stuck on the first riffle. They unloaded some of the goods today. It was an up river job, but the evening tide did not float the boat. It was good and warm today with the sun making up for lost time. Tried to get the [Quileute] Indians to go get the scow, but they did not like the idea. Jake down and took Nell, Tealie, Lucille, and myself to Quillayute for a ride. Clear. Nelson here.

1914 SUNDAY 31, MAY

Clear. Tealie went to Forks about noon. The boys tried this morning to bring the *Rhody* up but she went on another bar, so they will unload her where she is. Got dinner for the Indians. The *Rhody* came up on this evening tide. Floyd went out and brought in the scow. I went to the beach with him. Morse's down on the *Skagit*. I went out in the tin boat. Jim Kay and a crowd from the [road] camp down. Clear. NW wind.

JUNE MONDAY 1, 1914

Clear. Henry Marshall down for silo lumber. J.M. Smith was down with two teams yesterday. Thought the scow was in. Scow unloaded by the oil house.

Not much doing today. Floyd took Nell, Cile, Tealie, and myself down the river intending to take us out the mouth but it was rather rough. They all

Rhododendron and *Pearl* at Mora

got to throwing water, and as usual I got wet. Tealie, Floyd, and Lloyd went to the cannery to skate. Cloudy. Took scow down to LaPush.

1914 TUESDAY 2, JUNE

Heavy wind most all night. Rather threatening weather. Floyd wired A.T. [Albert T. Johnson] asking to leave scow, permission granted. Went down to go out. Mrs. Morse and Lucille along, also Ned [Clark]. Ned fell in the river. Mrs. M[orse] and I went up the river. The youngsters went to meet Charley. Not much mail. Cloudy. The *Rhody* raced with the *Sol Duc* and beat her.

JUNE WEDNESDAY 3, 1914

Cloudy. Heavy wind last night. Baked. W.F. went to the ranch. Not much doing. Lloyd and I made up orders and got them ready for Floyd. Went to LaPush with Floyd when he left. Took some pictures. Floyd went straight to sea, looked as if he might run into nasty weather the other side of Umatilla [lightship]. Walked up from LaPush. Cloudy.

1914 THURSDAY 4, JUNE

Clear. A very good night after all. Nell, Cile, Tealie, and I rode up as far as Eb's in the cart, from there Gretta, Tealie, Cile, and the children rode to the school house.[40] The exercises were held in the church [next door] and were very good. The little Smith children did fine. The crowd had a lunch at the schoolhouse and enjoyed themselves very much. Betty came down with the girls. Clear. We sprung the axle on the old cart.

Boats off James Island

1914 Thursday 11, June

Clear. Al down with Mrs. Sult and a stranger. Lloyd came home. The Hosacks have arrived, are up at John Hermanson's. The girls down. Al gave us a ride. Four of us rode up til we met Charley. All of us walked from Quillayute P.O. Eb and Marjorie up to meet Frank M[orse]. Frank must have had a miserable trip, seasick without supper at Clallam and the long stage ride in.[41] Nell and Cile up to meet her. Clear. Jim [Clark] went to the ranch on his way to Jackson Creek.

Quillayute Prairie school group. Wesley Smith on left. Tealie in white bonnet and dress.

1914 FRIDAY 12, JUNE

Clear. Gretta and the children just went home last night after several days at the cannery. George had a big time. W.F., Mr. Elliott [Jefferson County Road Supervisor], Jim Clark, Mr. Ferguson, and Mr. Yates are laying out a trail to the Hoh River. Jake called up while Tealie was at the cannery. Everybody skating, S.G. said.

JUNE SATURDAY 13, 1914

Frank expected her trunk, come to find out she did not get it checked. Just had it brought down to the dock thinking it would follow without even a name on it. They are joking her a lot about it.

Frank Morse

JUNE WEDNESDAY 17, 1914

Clear. Went into Forks for engine hood. Run into a nasty rut on Quillayute. Got home 3:45 a.m. Did not get up till after nine. Lloyd and Al washed and repaired the car. Al had a nasty headache. Billy Raymond and family down to return call. Mrs. Raymond saw the ocean for the first time. Al, Tealie, and I went fishing. Al and Tealie took the fish to Forks. Got back about 12, did not run into any wagons. A bunch of [the] boys from the [road] camp down. Clear.

1914 THURSDAY 18, JUNE

Clear. The girls came up early to go to Forks. Cile a regular clown. Al and Lloyd caught 14 fish. Al went back to Forks, brought [George] Siegfried and Mrs. Sult down to Maxfield's after strawberries. Jakie [Hahn] here for the girls. They came back about eleven, as Jakie could not bring them down tomorrow night. Dr. Woods stayed all night, going out in the morning. Nell, Frank, and Cile stayed all night.

1914 SATURDAY 20, JUNE

Clear. Gretta gave birth to twin girls. Jean and George came down in auto. Nell and Cile up to meet them. Tore up a blanket to make diapers. Sammy asking everyone for old clothes for the babies. Cile and Nell put ice down Charley's neck. Lloyd and Tealie went to Forks, Al and Jakie down. Mr. Brety and a young man here, walked up the beach on their way to Neah Bay. Rainy.

JUNE SUNDAY 21, 1914

Rain. One of the twin girls died this a.m. Hugh on way to cannery to make coffin. I got busy and made a little dress and skirt. Used Tealie's small doll to fit them on. Used silk that I got to make Tealie's dress for the 4th. Has not rained since about eleven this a.m.

1914 MONDAY 22, JUNE

Frank stayed here with Jean and George while the others went to the funeral. I went up with Eb. Gretta feeling fine and baby doing well. Walked back. Cloudy.

JUNE TUESDAY 23, 1914

Clear in spots. Lloyd and I went to Forks with Al, came back just ahead of Charley. Lloyd took the car and took Nell, Tealie, and Frank up to Eb's. Gretta just fine. Lot of postcards came, also riding skirt, Cile's new hat and coat; think they will look fine on Cile. Have had Colty and Snokums up all day, put the saddle on Snokums. Rainy.

Lloyd Taylor

1914 WEDNESDAY 24, JUNE

W.F. and Lloyd cut the hay across the road just the last of this month. Smith and Kidd and Marshall have a Ford car each. Toler spent most of the ten days before the 4th in here selling Fords. [John] Grader's Cadillac is a fine looking car but I imagine the expense of upkeep will be great in this country.

JULY FRIDAY 3, 1914

Lloyd came in with his car, as far as Forks.

1914 SATURDAY 4, JULY

Lloyd came down and decorated the car [for the 4th], took S.G. and the girls up to Forks. Jake down after Tealie. The cars came back and forth all day. Curtis and Ern down with the Morse girls and Mrs. Meredith. Ray [Shamley] driving the Forks Hotel car. He invited me to go up with him. There were 7 grown folks and 4 children. Had a blow out just the other side of the prairie. Ern came along and helped put on a new tire.

[The next entry is the following:]

1914 SATURDAY 1, AUG

The World Afire.[42]

SEPT. WEDNESDAY 9, 1914

Charley [Palmer] and Beth married today. Lloyd and I are going to take them to Angeles, also Mr. [Charles] Fulmer. Al took part of the crowd. Walt

Lake Crescent ferry

took Beth and Charley to Forks. We had old shoes, cow's bells and numerous articles on the car. Blew out a tire about two miles the other side Sloan's camp. Someone had taken the pump so had to go to the lake on the rim. Expected to meet George but he was still at the lake. Almost dark when we got across with the *Betty Earls* [Lake Crescent ferry].

Thursday – [In route to Seattle]

Floyd started for Washington Harbor with a scow loaded with a camp outfit, eight men and a woman cook. It got pretty rough off Dungeness, the woman got so sick she wanted to jump overboard. I got sick and went to bed, did not wake up till we were by the rock inside the Harbor. Tealie had been sick too.

Sept. Friday 11, 1914

The people on the scow went ashore for breakfast. We cooked breakfast aboard. When the tide was high took scow around in front of Main's and let it drift ashore where they unloaded it. Took *Rhody* over to the other side of the bay away from the wind and anchored. In the evening went over to the store and got some supplies. Got the scow off and started out. Got dark on us before we got out of the bay. Had supper ready but had to wait till we got to anchor off Protection [Island]. The tide was running so hard had to lay there till three o'clock [a.m.].

1914 Saturday 12, Sept.

Got into Seattle about four o'clock p.m. All cleaned up and the boys shaved, took Les so long that the whiskers grew out on one side before he got the other side shaved. When I got out on the after deck to wash and comb my hair, I know that we passed every liner and gas boat that was outward bound that day. Went out to Hat's [Aunt Hattie Hildebrand].

1914 Tuesday 22, Sept.

Left on the *Rhody* for home [from Seattle].

Sept. Friday 25, 1914

General Hospital at Angeles burned. Cile alright.

Oct. Wednesday 7, 1914

Still trying to wash but engine is on the bum again. Too damp for clothes to dry any way, but everything is dirty so must get some washing done. Politicians galore are finding their way to Western Clallam, it is their hunting season [for votes].

1914 Thursday 8, Oct.

Rainy, as it has been for most of the time. Just plain Oregon drizzle. Bertha [Lawrence Palmer] and Walter [Palmer] down and stayed all night. Lloyd came in bringing Mrs. Morse, S.G., and Lucille, who is looking much better. Lloyd has his new light on and they are fine, looks like a big car now.

1914 Saturday 10, Oct.

Partly clear. Lloyd and Tealie went to Forks, may go on to Clallam to a dance. A Ford and an Overland from Port Townsend here. They walked to the beach, say they enjoyed themselves fine. Beth and Charley with the mail. [Walt and Chas. Palmer have the mail contract for

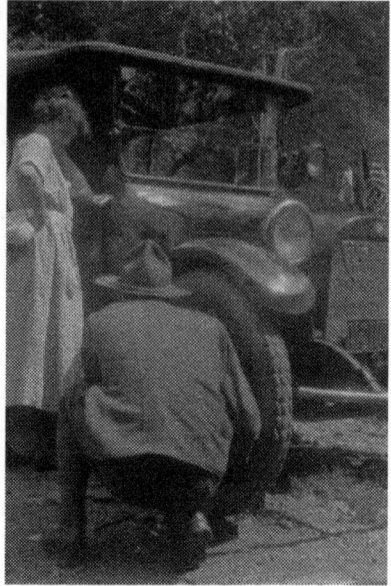

Working on automobile

another term, as of 9-4-14]. Beth can drive pretty well now.

1914 Monday 12, Oct.

Rained and blew all night. The river is up some and is getting quite muddy. Harvey [Smith] down with the children [Betty and Zona], both of them seemed to have a good time. Not many at the Clallam Bay dance. Mrs. [Florence] Jeter worse. Has rained hard all day. Harvey gave us a goose, which we had for dinner.

Dec. Sunday 20, 1914

Clear and cold. Mr. And Mrs. K[eene] and myself went over to the lake. Walked the full length on the ice. Skating would have been fine. Capt. A.J. Smith and Mrs. Tyler[43] were down to the beach. The first time the old man has been to the beach for some years. Three successive Sundays have been clear and cold.

1914 Friday 25, Dec.

Had Christmas dinner at Morse's, Tealie and I. There was Eb and family, Hugh and Marjorie, George Siegfried and Frank Batalph. It rained all day and my cold made me feel miserable. George [Morse] was scared really into hysterics when Santa (Frank Batalph) opened the door, he finally shook hands with Santa, but was relieved when Santa's mask came off and revealed

Skating on lake, Mrs. Keene and Quileute man not mentioned in Dec. 20 entry

Frank. Jean did not like his looks either. After a big dinner, I came home. George and Frank came, Frank to do the chores and George to go up after Mr. and Mrs. Sult. All the crowd went to LaPush but W.F. and myself.

My cold was getting worse and my lungs were getting pretty sore. So I doctored all-night and set up most of it. Saturday Mr. and Mrs. Sult, Dr. Brown and Mr. Huston came up from LaPush and George took them home. My cold is still pretty bad. Seems as if the weather man had it in for us, lovely weather for three weeks and rain all day Christmas, clear the next day. Ivor [Iverson] down after gasoline. Eb and Gretta went up home. Marjorie went to Joe's [Marsh]. [44] Slow work this taking care of a cold. Santa brought me a gold thimble, a Moqui water jug, a book, fine box of candy, motor bonnet, fine handkerchiefs, hand painted vase, an embroidered towel.

1914 Tuesday 29, Dec.

Charley wanted to go to the [Christmas] tree at Smith's. Charley hauled fish all day Sunday. Quite a heavy mail Tuesday both in and out. 5 sacks going out. Walt at Forks with extra load. Everyone came home, the single men beat 55 to 32 — they must have been hoodoed to let that bunch beat them. Gretta and the children went to Keene's to spend a day. Mr. K. had a hard time getting up the river because of the wind. Mr. K was cursing for the first time here.

Dec. Wednesday 30, 1914

Margaret Orrett[45] and her friends went to Angeles today. [John] Grader was here to meet them. Gretta came up in the afternoon and went up with

Cannery boxes and women in background

George [Siegfried] in the car. George had brought down two Indians. He wanted Tealie and I to go up with him. Could not go. Went to bed early, but could not sleep good.

1914 THURSDAY 31, DEC.

Frank and Hugh went up to Eb's. Lots of fish today. Walt has made three trips and has two to make yet. Sammy [S.G.] wants Eb to come down and work tomorrow so he will be able to work all the year. There was to have been a moving picture show at Forks tonight but the movie man failed to appear. Tealie went to Forks with Karl [Carl] Wahlgren, there is to be a masquerade. Walt brought down ½ ton of sugar.

Chapter 2

Datebook for 1915

Taholah – Photo by Fred Bartram[46]

1915 Friday 1 January

The sun shining, by noon a beautiful New Years day. Joe Pullen up buying for a big feed, the Quinault's gave the money. Those that went to Taholah had a big time, a big potlatch, so Joe said. Jack Hudson not to be outdone is also buying for a feast. Walt [Jackson] hauled fish till after one o'clock last night.

January Saturday 2, 1915

George Siegfried came in about 8 o'clock p.m. on his was to the cannery. About nine two cars full came and went to LaPush to the dance, they came back about two. During the latter part of the night it began to blow and rain. This morning when George, Nell, Mrs. Morse, and Frank left it was raining and blowing hard; they had a bad day for their trip. Everyone reports a nice time at the dance at LaPush.

Made out quarterly account and stamp account. Am going to write another page or two to Mrs. Reagan.

Charlie Howeattle came in on the stage. Answered memory lesson and wrote to Mrs. Reagan. *American, Everybody's, Hearsts, Cosmopolitan,* and *Worlds Work* came on the mail. Have not looked at the papers yet. Cloudy but not raining.

January Monday 4, 1915

Clear for a while then clouded up and began to sprinkle. Eb went down to the cannery. School began again today. Very near made an apron, would of gone to Gretta's if it had not rained. Quite a lot of Indians here today, Arthur [Howeattle] got a canoe load of hay. Carl [Black] got a load of supplies, George [Siegfried] and Charlie [Hagadorn] down with both cars.

Marjorie[47] and Chick [Griffith] came down with Joe's [Marsh] buggy in time to take Nell home from school.[48] Hugh had gone down earlier in the day.

Conrad Williams mailed a bear hide to Weil Bros, postage $1.44, that seems rather steep as furs are so low in price that the postage will eat up all the profit. The Indians have a few sealskins, but they are too heavy to ship east and they have to be shipped green. Cold.

1915 Tuesday 5 January

Clear again for a wonder, hope it stays like that for all day. Sewed for an hour or two, do so little sewing that I cannot accomplish much in an hour. Mr. Ferguson down after mail, wanted to know who the Santa was that remembered him with the moccasins. Hugh says there are 17 boxes of fish so Charley will be down with the team. Arlie called up and said George [Siegfried] and he were coming down. Nell is not going up as her face is enlarged on one side. That tooth of Nell's will be good for as many visits to Angeles as mine were. Quite a lot of mail, Charley nearly as early as with the car. Got his mail ready about 11 o'clock; it will take him till seven in the morning to get thru to Tyee. Pretty cool but not freezing.

January Wednesday 6, 1915

Clear. W.F. gone to the ranche, went over with the Orrett boys. [Walter] Ferguson will go in a day or two. Two numbers of *Pearsons* came in last night.

Asked Nell if she and Gretta would go to Rixon's [at Westlands on the Sol Duc River] if I would call George up. She did not say anything so I called Gretta up and then we got George on the phone and arranged a trip for after supper. Mrs. [Caroline] Rixon had gone to bed when we got there but she got up quick. We had a very pleasant evening. Coming back I had to walk up the last of the Soleduck Hill. On the Quillayute hill had to turn at the gravel pit and back up the hill.[49] Gretta was worried for fear she would have to walk. Did just get around the house. Snowing on Quillayute—cold.

January Friday 8, 1915

Read most of the afternoon. Tealie cooked one supper and I cooked another.

Tealie made two caps. Mrs. [Arilla] Johnson sent in a hand painted pin for myself, Floyd sent a handkerchief, on last night's mail [Fannie's 42nd birthday on the 13th]. Cool, showers.

January Sunday 10, 1915

Rained most all night. Mr. Keene got his roller skates, expect he will be kicking high.

Filled out blank asking for p.m. [Post Master] appointment. Only two blanks came in. Wrote to Hon. Albert Johnson. Have several more political letters to write.

Not much out going mail. The wind has calmed down some. Hal [George] came up and fed Colty and Snokums.

January Tuesday 12, 1915

Raining as usual. Cleaned up my letters, went through them and answered all that were unanswered. Hugh brought Marjorie's trunk up and put it in the warehouse. Charley is coming with the team tonight. Nell went down and could not get her boat over the mud flat so she came back and stayed for the mail and had supper. S.G. is better.

S.G. and Lucille Morse

Invoice from Sellers for the cut glass sugar and cream set. It did not cost any more than the Eastern houses charge for that class of goods.

Read the papers until I nearly froze and was just making up the mail when Charley got up to feed his horses.

Pretty cold and raining. Snow on the ground this morning, did not last.

January Thursday 14, 1915

Fairly decent day, all but the wind. Tealie and I dressed and got all ready to go to the beach last night, but backed out when we got down to the river and saw how dark it was. Came back and spent the evening reading.

Nell and Hugh here for supper. Swen [Svere Johnson] down with load of mail, had a flat tire. Took it off, put in new tube, and an extra casing. Tire was flat again in a few moments, but he went to Forks that way. Came back with second load of mail about two o'clock.

Cut glass creamer and sugar bowl that Nell and Tealie ordered came in tonight. Not just exactly what was ordered but very nice. Sent out three sacks of mail. Cold.

January Saturday 16, 1915

Got up late, the sun was shining and it had been pretty cold all night. Tealie got breakfast. After breakfast Tealie went to the cannery. W.F. went also. About one Walt came down after fish, bringing Dr. Koenig with him [Forks Dr.]. W.F. and S.G. came to an agreement regarding hotel business.

Walt came with the mail about half past. Tealie and myself went to LaPush to watch the [Quileute] Indians play basketball. The girls were playing when we got there. Tealie played in the last half, Mrs. K[eene] played both.

The schoolboys played after which the older ones played a game. Simon Jones and Roy Black are sure doing fine. We walked back after the game; Jack Ward and Daniel [White] came up, as they had to use our boat. Cold and clear.

1915 Sunday 17 January

Cold and clouding up as if for a snow; about two the sun came out nice and bright. Hal [George] starts for school [at Chemawa Indian Boarding School]; going to Port Angeles with [John] Grader and Tealie.

Ivor [Iverson] and his father down. Mr. Keene brought up my baskets yesterday and they are fine. Mrs. Morse up and spent a couple hours. I always enjoy her visits. Walt down and took up a load of fish, guess this will be the last for a while unless prices go back to normal.

[George] Yates was here with a petition for a footbridge across the Quillayute. Also took up the question of his buying into the store, but he has not the money.

Finished reading *Cosmopolitan* and wrote three letters; have a lot to write yet, but have made up the mail and intend to go to bed. Cold and clear.

JANUARY WEDNESDAY 18, 1915

The *Pearl* off LaPush — nice and clear. Ferguson was down and helped get the hardware room ready for the new load. Flour is retailing at $2.15 in Seattle Guy [Lesure] says. I know it must be near $8 a dbl. whole sack by now.

Mrs. She-set-cop[50] and Susanna were up to get Hal's trunk which he left, taking his things in a suitcase.

Floyd and Guy had supper; it had been too rough to cook outside. Floyd has his small powerboat along as they did not think the *Pearl* could get up the river.

1915 TUESDAY 19 JANUARY

Clear and cold. After breakfast the boys went down to the cannery and brought up two boat loads; the *Pearl* cannot come up the river very well, at least they do not like to try as she might go aground.

Had four of the Indians here for lunch as it took longer to unload than if the boat lay off here. Began reading "The Hallow of Her Hand" by McCutcheon. Like it very well so far.

JANUARY WEDNESDAY 20, 1915

Clear. Oscar Wahlgren brought down two men traveling for the West Coast grocery of Tacoma. That is a good house but hardly profitable for us because of freight.

Nell stopped in on her way home from school; said Frank would be back home [from high school] by Sat. About twenty minutes after she went Grader came and had both Tealie and Frank, the folks were surprised. Frank was pretty tired, although she had spent a lively day. Eb went up home taking Gretta's wool cards. Cold and clear.

1915 THURSDAY 21, JANUARY

Clear. Bought a fish from Mark Williams [*Sa-wha-thlu*]. Tried to catch some chickens but the turkey gobbler interfered. He will go into the pot if he is not careful. Sally [Williams] came in and visited awhile. Fan [Morse] and Lucille up, Fan is going to Angeles with Wesley [Smith], who said he would be down by two and did not get here till after four. The two girls, Tealie and I went down to the lake, they had never been there before. Fan and I came right back, Tule and Tealie lost their way and had a great time coming back. Wesley went out with a flat tire and on two cylinders; do not think I would care to ride with [him], he shakes hands with the many stumps. Walt [Palmer] early with the mail, reports a tree fell on Jake's bridge smashing it so teams could not cross. Took out some fish. Cold and clear.

Two of Fannie's dogs

1915 SATURDAY 23 JANUARY

Cold. A few clouds ambling around, but cleared up by noon. S.G. has quite a few fish again today, hope he does well with these. Tealie went down to the cannery. Hugh said they skated, played basketball, football, one old cat, and some things he did not know what they were called. K.O. came in and went down to the cannery. Guess he came in to see S.G. about the hotel proposition.

The post card albums and one photo album came in on the mail, filled one of the P.C. albums. Received correction form [from] the P.O. auditor and they owe me the $12.00 instead of my owing them $45. If the department used adding machines such mistakes on their part could not occur.

Keene's order was paid Dec 21-14. Sears Robuck will have to dig up. Some of the folks are going to LaPush – Cold, bright moonlight.

1915 MONDAY 25 JANUARY

Clear, still freezing. W.F. went to the ranche taking Laddie. The other two wanted to go and for a wonder Teddy was willing to get into the canoe.[51]

Hugh [Morse] got a box of groceries and put them in the hall as he is going up the river tomorrow. Must be going to build a new house on his place.

Tealie went up and got 2 quarts of cream. Coming back Mr. Smith showed her a mouse that he had found in a nest 8 feet underground. He is going to take it home and see if he can thaw it out.

Have been setting around the fire talking tonight.

Cold and freezing – a few clouds.

January Tuesday 26, 1915

Cold and clear. David [Hudson] up and bought quite a lot of groceries. Gave him a pair of skates for Willie [David Hudson's son William]. Tealie cleaned up her accumulation of dishes. Mrs. Yakaladi [Jennie Obi] came with some clams, bought them as I do not like to turn them away when they travel so far to get them. Had scalloped clams for dinner and they were fine, almost as good as oysters.

Nell, S.G., and Lucille were here for dinner. Nell ate the healthiest she has for some time. The three girls went to the lake and did not get back till after dark - [they] came out behind the barn, and were full of devil's club briars. They ran into a half frozen snake and were nearly scared to death.

January Saturday 30, 1915

Clear, but clouded up towards night and during the evening rained. Tealie, Nell, and Lucille went to LaPush to spend the night [at] Keene's. All took their roller skates.

World's Work, *McClures*, *Hearsts*, and *Everybody's* came in tonight so have a lot to read. Received a letter from Mrs. Swaustrom and she took Tealie for me in the picture. Maybe I did look like that once. She says Lloyd looks just like she thought he would.

A card from Qapah, [*Ibapah*] Utah, from Mrs. Reagan, they have been transferred [from Nett Lake]. I know she wrote me in August that they would quit the service if a suitable transfer was not forthcoming. Raining.

1915 Sunday 31 January

Clear again but clouded up during the day and rained a little. George [Siegfried] down and went to the cannery. Walt [Palmer] and four of his brothers went to the beach. George and Nell and Tule and Tealie went to Forks. Gretta and the children went home; they went to the cannery yesterday.

The black paper to make my album for panoramas came in today; cut and put extra pieces on quite a number of leaves. It is going to be quite a job to fix those but it is the only way as albums for no. 4 panoramas are not made any more.

George [Siegfried] and the girls stayed all night. They certainly had a good time and you should see Tule's midday; she swept the floor with it. It was eleven o'clock before I could get them to bed. Folks around Forks would not know George if they could see him down here. Raining.

One of Fannie's many panoramas "Mouth of the Quillayute River West Coast Clallam Co. Wash."

1915 TUESDAY 2 FEBRUARY

Raining. Made up my money order report. Read some. Have my big photo album finished and prints mounted, it is an improvement to having them lay around loose.

Yesterday Tealie and I worked our heads to the extent of planning what we would do if we got the old Ford from Lloyd. We worked out the sketch of a plan for a trip to the California fairs and the Grand Canyon, as I would never get that close and not see it. Come to think of it I have been closer than San Diego is, when we were in Colorado and Utah. We could just as well [have] went through the southern route, but a dollar always looks like a cartwheel to W.F.

Nell stopped for supper. Frank came up. John Grader came down and took Tealie to the basketball game.

FEBRUARY FRIDAY 5, 1915

Cloudy. Tealie and Frank got breakfast. The sheep go to the island and stay all day, the feed must be better.

W.F. went to the ranch and took Gyp, poor little thing she hates to be left behind so. Harvey came and went to the beach. Tealie and Frank went to the cannery. John Sailto surprised me by coming in and paying his bill. I was never so surprised. Charlie Howeattle got a padlock for his canoe, says he intends to keep it locked up, it must have been getting on the wrong side of the river. Cut out four middy blouses and made one today. Three are of Krinkle Kloth, the kind we will want on our trip. I believe that kind of goods would be fine for bloomers too. Have been looking through *Automobile* to find a car and cannot get past a Ford.

1915 SATURDAY 6 FEBRUARY

Blew and rained hard most all night. Susie came up to wash this morning, she says it blew hard at LaPush last night and the river is up some this morning.

Eb drove Red down and went to the cannery. Harvey is down after some of his sheep, took all but thirty-eight home. Sheepa had a lamb last night, the first this year.

Hugh took a sack of oats over and fed the horses.

Bertha and Walt [Palmer] down with the mail, had supper with Tealie and myself.

My box came from Huntleys, everything O.K. but Lucille's ring did not come, will be in later. It was a six I ordered instead of a seven. The cut glass is just like diamonds and the pins are just right. Not many here for their mail tonight. Cloudy.

Sunday Feb 7, 1915

Clear. Tealie telephoned to Nell and Tule asking them to come up and we would go to the old Morganthaler[52] place back of the lake [between Mora schoolhouse and Quillayute Prairie]. The trail is grown over with salmonberry bushes and getting through leaves many marks. The girls wore bloomers and I was wishing for a pair before I got through. I have a light pair of shoes and in addition to wetting my feet, make me pretty tired. The old place is so grown over with salmon brush and blackberries that you can hardly push your way through from one building to another. The old barn looks the same as it did the time of my last trip over there. Two years ago Tealie and I were over to the old place and picked strawberries, wild ones. I do not suppose there are any plants left now. Some of the apple trees have broken limbs, most likely done by the bears. The house is in a good state of preservation. Around the doors and windows the sills have rotted some, but the log part is still good. We went up stairs and found nothing had been there since we were.

The girls posed in one of the windows and I took their pictures. The old rose bush has not made the luxuriant growth most of the old roots have. Out in the alder tree I took some more pictures of the girls, took Lucille going and coming. We came back to the old cannery road and cut across lots to the cannery, from there S.G. came over and got us. Mrs. Morse had dinner at three; George Clark and Charlie Hagadorn were down to see Hugh. Tealie got good and wet when she took one of the boats across.

Nell, Lucille, and Tealie in Morganthaler window frame

1915 MONDAY 8 FEBRUARY

Clear again. Heard Susie out in the shed splitting wood before I felt like getting up, but up it was. S.G. and Conrad [Williams] came along on their way up the river to Hugh's place. They took Klahn's and Ferguson's mail, all but a register for the old lady.

Tried to catch a chicken but the barred rocks all know that it is speckled chicken I want and they stay on the other side of the bunch.

Susie washed. As the day was nice I went to LaPush and took both of my cameras. The sun is just fine. I was very much surprised to find the big log sawed out of the road and to find farther down a big pile of puncheons. Looked as if someone must have been breaking the reservation laws, hope the offence was bad enough to fix a lot of road.[53]

Found May [Hudson or Hobucket] just putting Doris [Keene] to bed for her nap. As I wanted some pictures of the schoolhouse I went to the top of the outside stairway and took two. It was a splendid place to get a picture as all the street north facing the ocean and out a ways to sea was included in one picture. The second picture, the schoolhouse is in the extreme right and the

Lucille, Tealie, and Nell in alder tree.

ocean has most of the stage. I took two of the pupils. The youngsters were so anxious to sit where you wished, that speak to one and the whole bunch jumped up.

The ocean was grand today, a fast heavy swell showing that the wind has been blowing fast and furious somewhere lately. The breakers were rolling with long streamers of spray following them. They reminded me of a locomotive with the smoke streaming out behind it. I took pictures galore of it, went close to the surf, but the white mist that always hangs along shore when a heavy sea is running may dim them up some. With the small camera I took Kenneth with the surf for a background.

I tried to get little Harvey Eastman to let me take a picture of him but he took to his heels. I would like very much to get a picture of him to send to Gordon [Hobucket]. He looks so different [from] the other youngsters at LaPush.

Took two pictures of Mrs. David Hudson [We-ba-stub or Ella], she was making baskets, beside her stood the white cross and stand of the Shakers. It was not very light but I threw the stop open and gave [it] a second. I think that was plenty of time. Also I got a picture of the wooden fireplace in old Mason's house. I know what would happen to that fireplace if I tried to keep a fire in it, it would burn up. Took a likeness of the un-heavenly twins John Sailto and Jimmy Hobucket.

Kenneth Keene

Frank Bennett has 40 days on the road so the logs are sawed out and a lot of puncheon has been made, by the time he gets done the road to LaPush will be pretty good.

Came home and made some buckwheat cakes; Nell stayed and ate with me. Sheep came up by themselves tonight. Cloudy.

1915 WEDNESDAY 10 FEBRUARY

Clear. Susie came to wash, this makes two days this week so far. Tealie and Frank went to the upper end of the Quillayute Prairie with George, stopped at Gretta's on the way back and came home when school was out. Nell and I went to the cannery and Tealie and Frank came in about an hour. We stayed till after nine.

Today was Nell's birthday — 20 years old [2/10/1895], the girls began calling her the old maid. When George [Siegfried] came he brought pictures of Lucille and Tealie in their baseball suits.

John Sailto and Jimmy Hobucket

Cold and clear. Susie finally finished the washing tonight. We have not had things well cleaned up before for three months, it has been so difficult to get clothing dry. Took down most of the clothes tonight as it may blow and scatter them all over the place.

THURSDAY FEB 11, 1915

Clear. Yesterday was Nell's birthday and today was George junior's — Nell is 20 and George five. Mrs. M. and S.G. went up [to Gretta and Eb's]. Mrs. M. walked and S.G. went

Mason chimney

George's photos of Tealie (left) and Lucille (right) in baseball suits (February 10).

with Marshall. Walt has taken up 10 boxes of fish already. (5 o'clock). Gretta and the children down when Marshall came for gasoline. I am glad the cut glass creamer and sugar arrived in time. The joke is that Nell picked it out herself thinking it was for Mrs. Sult.

Lucille has been under the weather some as a result of her trip Sunday—that and laying on her stomach on the ice. She needs exercise but not too strenuous. It is hard for her to realize that she cannot go the limit.

Today Mr. Marshall brought Frank, Lee, George Jr., and Jean down for a ride and to get S.G. Took a picture of the children and of S.G., Jean, and George. Mr. Morse is more feeble than I thought, he uses a cane and leans on it more heavily than I like to see.

Saturday February 13, 1915

Have been making out an order for post cards for next summer's trade and find it will take about $70 worth to start the summer. This should be a good year as the road being open to the lake [Crescent] will bring a good many tourists down.

S.G. Morse and Frank Marshall in front, Lee, Jean, and George Jr. in back

In the last week have sent in 5 rolls of film. I took a number of the surf last Monday, as the sea was wonderful. So wonderful that $2,500,000 went down in the Columbia jetty. Just the swells were running half way to the top of Cake Rock. The sea came from almost direct south.

Some big vessel was making an awful racket off shore this morning. The whistling stopped short off. It does not seem as if fog could have been the reason as the signaling would gradually die away in the distance. Guess no one was hurt or the Indians would of spoke of it.

Fawcett [E.M. Fassett] and [Walt] Ferguson [both assistant engineers] are working on the road survey from the Mora schoolhouse up the river, and intend before finishing to locate the road to the cannery. The people on the river need and should have a good road that a car can travel over. The river was very well in times gone by, but the country is rather well along in years to be still using that primitive way of travel — the canoe.

The President has served notice that a special session will be called to pass the ship purchase bill if the present congress fails to do so. The purchase bill has been placed ahead of the appropriation bill and as a result local employees of the Interior Department have not been paid for nearly two months. And such proceeding make hard sledding for some of them, as the average salary paid does not leave much margin for putting aside for a rainy day. Uncle Sam gives you section hand wages for a scientific education, so if you miss a payday your credit suffers.

FEBRUARY MONDAY 15, 1915

The sheep are getting [so] they want to stay out nights and I do not like that.

Two of the [Quileute] Indians, Conrad and Mark [Williams] came up and mailed three seal skins to New York. Billy [Hudson] mailed his to the Hudson Bay [Fur] Co. in Seattle and think he is wise. It takes so much to pay the postage to the 8th zone [postal zone over 1,800 miles] that there is not much left because the Eastern houses are not giving any better prices. Cool.

1915 TUESDAY 16 FEBRUARY

A raw rain. Mrs. [Mary] Sult came back in with [Ritchie] Kidd, Tealie stayed over.

SURF AT MORA, CLALLAM CO. WN.

Cake Rock (*chachalak.ᵂó·sat*) on left, Dahdayla (*dá·dila*) on right

Walt has to make two trips after fish; Nell and Lucille came down with [him], as did the piano man. Nell took one of the pianos; it is to be a surprise for Frank. Well, they will all get pleasure from it, as Nell likes to play.

Received prints of pictures that I took over at the Morganthaler place and of the Indian boys at LaPush. All are good.

FEBRUARY WEDNESDAY 17, 1915

Clear. Link Sands and the piano man brought down the piano Nell bought. [Link] Sands drove the team down this steep place at the end of the lane;

"The old and the new"

Group skinning seals.

four of them lifted it out of the wagon and put it on the canoes. Mrs. M. says they did not have a single mishap, but I think Nell got a second hand piano put off on her.

W.F. went to the ranch. Jake [Hahn] took Dr. Woods and the [Indian Affairs] Inspector [L.F. Michael] back to the top of the mountains where [Fred] Pool's team met them. I am to get Dr. a root of Scotch broom, don't want to forget it now.

Went to the cannery with Nell, had blueback for supper, it was just fine. Frank played the piano, Cile said she might of got a nightmare, told her that

Quileute Athletic Club at LaPush

the rest of us would think that we had one if she did, stayed at the cannery. Cold and clear.

1915 THURSDAY 18 FEBRUARY

Cold. Jim Clark and [Engineer R.W.] Remp were down looking over the road to the cannery. Bertha [Palmer] came down with Walt [Palmer] and stayed while he made a trip to Forks with fish. George called up. Cold.

FEBRUARY FRIDAY 19, 1915

Cold and Clear. Cliff [Wilson] is running the road between here and the prairie; it will be fierce till they get it dragged. They intend to fix the lane too while they are at it. Tomorrow Remp is going to survey the line to the cannery.

Perhaps Frank playing for Hugh Morse.

Dave [Hudson] brought up the big totem and gave it to me. Do not know what I shall do with it.

Went over and fed the horses, they were clear out of feed. Blacky had two lambs, found them both dead, that comes of my letting them stay out last night. Two nice little yews.

Tealie took her violin and went to the cannery for tonight. The *Smile* of Taholah came up today. Going back tomorrow. Cold and clear.

1915 SATURDAY 20 FEBRUARY

Cloudy. Jack Hudson came up early, says he is going to Taholah, [Norvel] Cope's Fourth of July, make $1,000.

Mrs. Rixon, daughter Gertrude, Miss [Esther] Bertolet, and Miss Hendricksen came down in the new Rixon auto, and walked on over to the [Rixon] ranch on Teahwhit Head.

The surveyors finished the line to the cannery today, went without dinner to do so.

Walt came and got a load of fish. George Siegfried came after the girls. Harvey came down to get four of the Indians to take them to the basketball game. Sequim got in about dark. Expect the folks will stay all night.

1915 MONDAY 22 FEBRUARY

Mrs. Rixon and party came back from Teahwhit Head, had a bunch and left for home about four.

Walt came for fish and there was only one box in, about an hour after he left [Morton] Peterson came up with a lot of fish.

Tealie went to the cannery and her and George [Siegfried] are still there. It is hard to tell where the four girls live, they rather divide their time between the two places.

Tealie playing violin. Note: the basket behind Tealie's left shoulder is the same basket pictured on Doris's head on p. 21.

Susie and May [Hudson] came down from Gretta's where they had been working. Talk about wet, they were in the hardest rain of the day and were drenched.

Some Indian just went past with a load of lumber, it is about eight o'clock. I'll bet he is wet. Got back money I gave to Hal [George] to go to school on.

The road machine made two trips over the road between Mora and the Prairie. The rain set in before it packed and now there are more ruts than ever. We have had such lovely weather that I guess Cliff did not look for any rain. If the rain had held off, the lane was to be fixed also.

A good many of the Quileutes have gone to Taholah to fish for Bluebacks. The *Smile* [of Taholah] came up and got Jack Hudson and family, also Roy Black went. The season is beginning very early and a big run is in sight.

Old Dave took the totem from S.G. and brought it up to me, then Mrs. Rixon came along and claimed it. Do not know as I want the big thing. It would have to be kept outside. If I could get another just the same height [I] would like them for gateposts.

David has his garden at his cabin [on the Quillayute River] all cleared up for plowing; he is sure a good gardener and likes to dig and plant.

Mrs. Rixon said she thought we could have filled several volumes if we had kept a close record while we were directors in [School District] 36. We both think Newbert would come back here to live if her and myself were to go on the school board.[54] He can be comfortable where he is, as neither one will tackle that particular job again. [Mrs. Rixon resigned from school district director on June 12, 1912. Fannie was the school district clerk in 1913.]

Joe Cole received a letter from Jonah this morning. I did not notice where he put it, but when he started to go a search failed to reveal the letter. He went through all his pants and overall pockets, looked in his purse and

The Rixon's were given the pole above and Fannie the *Tlokwali* house pole at top left. Both poles reside in the Smithsonian's curatorial facility.

Carl Black's street

the sack of hard tack he had just purchased, finally the letter was found in his shirt pocket. He is not so bad as Daniel White who is always losing his money and going thru all pockets but the one it is reposing safely in.

Have spent a part of the evening cutting out the jokes and Flossie Funnies from the *Ladies Home Journal.* I am going to make an album for each one. The cover pages I am going to mount in the big clothing catalogue. They will be fine to entertain visiting youngsters of the proper age.

FEBRUARY TUESDAY 23, 1915

Rainy. Received prints of schoolhouse views and they are splendid, even if the photographer does say so.

1915 WEDNESDAY 24 FEBRUARY

Raining. Walt came about seven for the mail. Tealie got breakfast for Nell so she could go to school.

Henry Marshall, Joe Marsh, and Eb [Morse] down. Frank Buttolph [Batalph] quit Eb last night. Do not see how he could be blamed.

Tealie and I made scrap books and photo albums most of the day.

S.G. brought us a leg of veal and some smoked blueback. More fat in the fish than in bacon.

Hunted the sheep, forgot till I got into the mud and wet that the woods was both wet and muddy.

Ella Hudson

The totem still decorate the front porch, and awaits an owner. The venerable gentlemen may be all of half a century but I doubt it. [Not sure whether she is speaking of Rixon's pole or hers.]

Received prints from Wischmeyer last night. The picture of the village and schoolhouse would be hard to beat. The street past Carl's [Black] and the one fronting the ocean are splendidly clear. The schoolhouse and playground is A no. 1. The pictures of the pupils are good, in spite of his bad intentions, Kenneth has a front seat in both. I tried to get him to get in front of the Indian children but he did not want his picture taken, but I have a front and rear view of him, both good.

Mrs. David Hudson [Ella or *Wa-bos-tob*] was a good subject, with the cross and bells very much in evidence. It is a fine example of the interior of a devout Shaker's home.

I was lazy and did not get up when Tealie rose to get Nell's breakfast so she could get to [Mora] school [to teach]. W.F. told Nell he would pay her to stay here so Tealie would get up in the morning. Nell said she would see how much Tealie would give her to stay at home. She would see who bid the highest.

February Thursday 25, 1915

Mrs. *She-Ste-cop* [Jennie Hudson] came up this morning with some baskets to sell, saying Hal did not have any money. Today I refused the baskets. In a little while she came back with a dollar and a half which she wanted me to send to Hal. I made out a money order and also put in $2.00 myself. She was so thankful because I fixed the letter up for her that she went down to the canoe and brought the baskets to me, cultus potlatch, [Chinook Jargon for a

Kenneth "front and rear view"

present or gift]. She did not know that I sent the $2.00 either. Some people are thankful for small favors. I do not think that the Indian women know how I appreciate the baskets they give me. I know that many of the gifts they potlatch to me are the best work they do.

1915 FRIDAY 26 FEBRUARY

Cloudy. W.F. took some oats and timothy seed, made Colty pack it and went to the ranch.

Tule liked her ring so well that she could hardly go to sleep because of it.

LaPush school house

Nell says I missed something when I did not see Lucille open the box and find her ring. She could not go to sleep worrying what she should do with it. Was unable to sleep with it on her finger and was afraid to take it off for fear the house would burn down and she would forget the ring. Lucille finds it harder than she thought it would be to forget the burning of the hospital and clothing and keepsakes.[55] Misty.

FEBRUARY SATURDAY 27, 1915

Cloudy. Tealie came up from the cannery. Took a notion to clean up and overhaul the front room. Brought down the sanitary couch from one of the upstairs rooms. All my tillacums, [Chinook Jargon for friends], here with clams. Bought some from Mrs. *She-ste-cop* and Mrs. [Emma] Cleveland gave me a mess of fine ones. Gave Walt [Palmer] the ones I bought for myself and also gave him some smelts.

George Siegfried came down in the afternoon. Tealie tried to get him to go on to the cannery, but he waited for the mail. Charley and Beth [Palmer] came down on the second trip with Walt [Palmer]. They are at Ed's [Smith] for supper so Mary tells me. Mary wants to buy a coat like Tealie's black one, but advised her to get a Balmacan, as it would be stylish and comfortable. Clear.

Woman with string of smelt

Lucille Morse circa 1920

Fannie on a river, probably while on vacation out of state, as this does not appear to be western Washington.

Sunday February 28, 1915

Have been watching the moon as it shines through the trees. When a youngster I would watch the moon till my eyes would ache, wondering what that same particular moon would look down and see me doing in the future. Tonight my dreams are backward and the only thing I can see is myself a youngster, dreaming dreams, not many of which have come true. Wonder if the future will realize them, maybe it will if I help. If not I can build castles in the air, I can have the fun of building them anyway.

A crowd of Indian boys have been doing prisoner work on the road, a result of a chicken supper the other night. Hoh Joe went up the river leaving the key to his house with Scott Fisher. Scott opened up the house and invited the boys in for a feed if they would rustle the chickens, which they did from several hen houses. As a result we are having some road improvements.

I think the method of punishment used on the reservation could be used to advantage with the white population.

A fine is not imposed as there would be very little likelihood of the culprit having any money to pay a fine; so he or she is fined so many days labor to be expended on government property or public improvements. And the Policeman has to see that the work is done.

MONDAY MARCH 1, 1915

Clear and warm. North wind. March on the coast came in like a lion.

Captain Saux [Wa-hub] and Jerry [Jones] came and got a load of hay. Morton [Penn] skinned the sheep that died last night on the trail.

The report is that the Washington Oil Company intends abandoning the present working and drilling somewhere else on the Forks Prairie. They may find oil. Too bad if they do not, as it would make awful liars of some of these geologists, which is what they are trying to make of one another.

Surf sounds as if there was a heavy sea. Clear and foggy.

1915 MARCH TUESDAY 2

Did the first sewing today that I have done for some time, put the plaiting on my black drop skirt. Then I got out the black overskirt and found it full of moth holes. That is the way in this country, one does not wear a fine dress often enough to keep the moths out. Will have to get a new top skirt, by the time I get done will be like the girl with the lavender belt. I like knock-about clothes too well for my own benefit. It is all very well to wear khaki middies and skirts because they are comfortable, but one can be so comfortable that keeping up appearances becomes a task to be dreaded. One gets to staying at home from many a social event because of being too lazy to dress properly. There are such things as clothes that are too comfortable.

My brush and comb set came in tonight. Have not heard from my books yet. Nell had some lunch and waited for the mail. Grader came down later and Tealie had to make biscuits.

The mail was in about 4:30 o'clock. Several magazines have come so far this month. Cloudy.

MARCH WEDNESDAY 3, 1915

Cloudy with rain towards evening.

Tealie in midday shirt and khaki skirt.

MARCH 4, THURSDAY 1915

Tealie and the Morse girls have quite a fad of wearing white stockings. Whenever S.G. is around he keeps them on the dodge by trying to put the end of his muddy cane on their white hose. There is one thing they have to keep them clean, and believe me it keeps them busy.

Walt down early with mail. S.G. up, but not feeling very well. Tealie's white sox in, Tule hid them and got one pair dirty. Postcards and prints of Quileute Day School came, sent some to Dr. Woods; also sent Mrs. Reagan and Mrs. Bartram pictures of Mrs. David Hudson and the athletic club. George Clark down says he thinks the biggest share of those oats will belong to him if he is to get half for half the work of planting. Clear.

Lucille in white

MARCH FRIDAY 5, 1915

Mrs. [Lillian Maxfield] Weldrick called up from Sappho and said Messers' Starbuck, Bricken, McDonald, and Steel would be here tonight. They came in about three o'clock in Weldricks 1910 five passenger Cadillac. Some more either suckers or planning to catch someone that is. Some more with wheels in their head who think there is some easy money lying around in here. If there were we would have it corralled ourselves; the inhabitants are not asleep. Some of them have been here long enough to be. There may be a fortune lying along this beach, but I imagine it will break a good many more before it is found. Whenever a good road goes down the beach, many of these places will be gold mines of another sort — Pleasure resorts. These beaches will be mined for something besides placer gold.

Mr. Elliott, road supervisor in Jefferson County, came in this p.m., accompanied by Frank Fisher and Howard Wheeler, after spending the day going over the trail between Hoh and Jefferson County line. The [Clallam] county engineer should have done this but has not yet. Now that the state has appropriated some money to be used in Western Jefferson, all trails are of interest and everyone is interested. The old Pacific Highway

Beach camp.

was surveyed 16 years ago, and is nearly all included in the Forest Reserve where it would be under Federal supervision if built. It crosses deep canyons and steep hills, while the proposed route along the beach would be scenic, with not over 5% grades and not any big bridges. Roads could be built down the river to it making a downhill haul and a good system of highways. Raining.

SAT. MAR 6, 1915
Cloudy, clear in spots.

Billy [Hudson] and David [Hudson] packed the Sunset men to the beach in a canoe and from there the two Indians are going to pack the bedding and a few days supplies to the mine. Two of the men besides Starbuck are miners, McDonald in Alaska and I have a hunch that Steel is a chemist, and it looks as if Brinker knew where he was traveling. If the money that has been spent on the Sunset had been used to work the kelp beds back of Ozette Island it would be yielding good returns by this time. Funny how the hopes of finding the yellow metal will warp the business judgement of so many. It is the eternal gambler that is in us all, and then we laugh at the Indians for wanting gold instead of a check or bill.

W.F. went with Elliott [Jefferson Co. road supervisor] to the beach and up the Dickey. S.G. went to the school meeting. When Walt [Palmer] came down Happy [Mary Smith], Benson, and I went to Forks with him. I went over and had dinner with Walt and Bertha [Palmer], as did the other two. We went to the Dungeness-Forks basketball game. Dungeness got beat 23 to 18 in favor of Forks. The girls took a chance on Grader or George. I went up with Walt on the mail car as did Mary and Benson. Grader broke down,

Nell driving next to George Siegfried. Appears to be S.G. and Susan Morse with Jean in back. Woman in white could be Lucille when ill.

could hardly get in from Angeles so it was up to George, and after walking over from Bogachiel he had to put in a new front spring so the girls and George did not get up to Forks till after the first half. Grader got them to hold the game till nine, but the first half was over when George got back.

The game resulted in favor of Forks 23 to 18. The visitors started roughing it from the first toss of the ball, and the Forks boys met them on their tactics the first half, 13 to 3 for Forks.

After the game the Forks boys entertained the visitors at a banquet at the Forks hotel. The Dungeness boys were a shamed face looking crowd before the evening was over, because they had played anything but a clean game and were beaten and treated like gentlemen.

We all stayed till after lunch. All had a good time. Benson wanted to come back with us but Harvey came just then. Harvey came near going into the ditch on his last trip. That steep bank is going to make trouble for some one yet. Wesley went and got the rest of the crowd. About nine o'clock George brought the Morse girls and myself home. Raining when we got home.

SUNDAY MARCH 7, 1915

Nell and I went to Forks with George when he took Mr. Elliott up. The sun was shining and it certainly was warm. Nell drove. I took both cameras.

Possibly George Clark and Martin Raun

When we drove up to Sults there came George Clark and Martin Raun. George with an eye tied up, "there, we should have taken him home last night," says Nell, for I know she thought the same as I did, George had been fighting. Instead of that he had been playing basketball and got an awful fall. The joke was he had the pork on his ear instead of his eye, guess it helped the eye alright. He and Tealie had taken Al's car and been riding all forenoon, neither one went to bed.

For the first time I was up to the top of Anderson's Hill. I took my big camera and four of us went over and took some pictures. It was sure warm. The day was fine for pictures and I got a good one, it took two exposures.

Some day I am going up above Ford's[56] and have a try at it, I understand you can see the ocean from there. We came down past Uncle John's place, the house has fallen down and it looks lonely. The last time I was there Mrs. Anderson and I packed chickens over because they were going after the raspberries. We used gunnysacks and went back and forth for three hours, but had a lot of fun.

Tealie and Grader came down about nine, shortly after Al and Harry Brooks [Storm King Resort] came, they had brought George Clark home. George [Siegfried] went to the cannery. Took up some groceries for Mrs. Sult.

1915 WEDNESDAY 10 MARCH

Clear in the a.m. S.G. called the girls up and told them to come and hang up the clothes. Fairly busy in the store.

[Sol Duc] Hot Springs car and Capt. J.A. Martin's car [Log Cabin Hotel] down. Jim and Mary [Clark] with them. Joe Pullen took them to the beach and back. Capt. Martin got stuck out by the warehouse. The lane is getting pretty bad.

Have rather neglected my writing the last day or two and must get busy.

It has been raining again. Susie came down from A.W.'s [Smith] where she has been washing. Will have her wash here to-morrow. Got up early to get Nell to School.

MARCH THURSDAY 11, 1915

Clear in spots. Walt down for fish and got stuck just at the gravel, took Tealie and I to pull him and push him out.

Fannie on Anderson Hill.

Susie washed and got some of our clothes dry.

George had dinner with us. Sven Johnson and Cliff [Wilson] came down with the mail.

Nell waited for the mail, and had supper while she waited. I received a letter from Mr. Reagan and was glad to hear that his new book [Don Diego] is at last for sale.

Raining.

1915 FRIDAY 12 MARCH

Tried and finally the sun shown. Susie working again today.

Dr. Woods went out with Walt. There were so many fish that Boyd Collins came down with a team about four and got twelve boxes.

Tealie, Nell, Lucille, & Frank plucking chickens.

Nell and Tealie boxed the fish for S.G. tonight.

Finished reading *"The Net"* by Rex Beach, it recalls the New Orleans incident that I remembered very well. Raining.

March Saturday 13, 1915

Walter brought in quite a load of mail, about time too as some of it has been on the road from Seattle for ten days. There is something wrong somewhere, either in the Seattle office, or the boat or between here and Clallam, and the worst of it is conditions are getting worse.

1915 Sunday 14 March

W.F. and Morton [Penn] came up from the ranch.

Raining and the river is good and muddy. Sven [Johnson] made three trips after fish, the last one about dark.

I took pictures of George and Nell by gaslight, just to use up the roll of film. I wish the panorama was ready to take off, as I want to see what kind of pictures I got of Forks Prairie.

Raining to beat the band.

March Monday 15, 1915

Remp and Ferguson down after a bill of groceries to start camp on the Dickey - Ozette trail. They will most likely be there for a couple of months

[at] the first camp. Al brought Remp down.

Not any fish caught today, the river reached the highest water of the season, about ten foot tide mark.

1915 TUESDAY 16 MARCH

Looks as if it would like to clear up. W.F. went to the ranch. Morton [Penn] went yesterday.

Harvey down with a drove of sheep. Little Betty helped him drive them.

Mrs. Smith and Zona in the buckboard. The first time Mrs. [Adeline Alexander] Smith has been down for several months.

Mail rig

1915 THURSDAY 18 MARCH

Cloudy. Arthur Howeattle in and sent out some furs. There has not been much trapping this year. The Indians sold the last years seal catch and did not average over $6.50 a piece for them.

George Clark, Billy Iverson, and Sven [Johnson] here. Billy brought the mail down as Walt broke an axle on his car yesterday mourning. George expects to leave day after tomorrow. Cloudy.

MARCH FRIDAY 19, 1915

Today promises to be our first good day for several days. The trouble with our weather this year is it has been too fine. Too much sunshine means forest fires in this country.

MARCH SUNDAY 21, 1915

Queenie and I slept in no. 1 [at Cottage Hotel]. I fell out of bed when I went to answer the bell.

I had my breakfast with Mrs. Sult. George Siegfried came down and I came along. Then we got all the girls and went back to Forks [Prairie] to take some pictures.

Forks Prairie – George Siegfried with camera

Nell, George, and myself walked from the cemetery to the old Ford place and then on up the hill [Fern Hill]. On a clear day you might be able to see the ocean from there but not today, as it was rather hazy. I think my pictures of the prairie itself were alright. I did not think there were as many fences on Forks as we had to go through on that place. Nell and I had a time with our narrow skirts. And it sure was hot, we near cooked getting back to the car. Mr. Wilson rode from just this side the forks of the road to Earl's road. George went back about ten. Clear.

1915 MONDAY 22 MARCH

Ned [Clark] was here running [survey] lines. K.O. was at the cannery last night and here this a.m. Morton [Penn] went to the ranch. They must have quite a little work done. It has been some time since I was down there.

1915 WEDNESDAY 24 MARCH

Clear. W.F. and Laddie went to the ranche, did not take much of a pack.

Wore my new high top shoes all forenoon and they did not tire my feet a bit. They fit fine.

Nell stayed all night. The rest of my music came, and the joke is on me, it is for the pipe organ. Mr. Sult had some good samples of oil from the Forks well.[57] Gerard and a new driller in.

MARCH THURSDAY 25, 1915

Clear. Got up and started Nell to school early. Last night I got quite a few things from Groffman [store]. Did not have anything for Nell to take for lunch.

1915 FRIDAY 26 MARCH

Clear. Yesterday was George Siegfried's birthday [3/25/1892], so tonight he is to have a supper at the cannery.

I have spent the afternoon sunning myself, it has been so fine.

An unusually quiet day for this kind of weather, not a single local car here except George.

The girls and George went to Forks tonight so as to start good in the a.m. Miss Bertolet is going with them from Sappho. Clear. Got a blueback from Chas. Howeattle [Pansy Howeattle Hudson's father].

MARCH SATURDAY 27, 1915

Clear. Feel some better this a.m. Phoned for butter and for Susie to come clean up. Susie wanted to go clam digging.

Fannie in high-top boots loading camera.
Note: Spruce Division Officer.

L. Orrett here and is waiting across the river for Margaret [Orrett], who will be down about mail time. David [Hudson] brought me some green onions, they look good. Susie finished in a hurry.

Frank [Morse] came up with S.G. for the mail. Walt asked us to go up with him to the basketball game, so I asked S.G. if Frank could go and he said yes. We stayed to the dance and so did Eb. Earl and Mary [Wilson] and Eb sat in the back seat, Frank sat on my lap.

When we got here I kindled a fire and it felt comfortable I can tell you. I sat and read till daylight. Rained in the latter part of the night.

MARCH MONDAY 29, 1915

Raining. Did not wake up till I heard someone at the door and was surprised to find it was ten o'clock. I was making up for lost time, as I did not get any sleep Sat. night. Charley [Palmer] came down with the team after fish, as Walt [Palmer] went to Clallam with the car.

Sherm was down with Eb's team and took up Mrs. Rixon's totem pole. Harvey put about 50 head of stock, he figures 120 acres will keep [them].

The Indians will not have any gardens left this year. [Harvey Smith's homestead was on the reservation side of the river and apparently not fenced.]

W.F., Morton, and Laddie came home. I made up the county bill. We are having a nice quiet rain, something that, strange to say, we needed. Read April installment of the "Honey Bee" in *McClure's*. All the cars but Billy's will be out tomorrow. Raining.

1915 TUESDAY 30 MARCH

Cloudy. Clear at times, but about noon clouded up. Mrs. Smith and her sister [Betty Alexander] down, Mrs. S. drove the car. Harvey bringing the sheep. He has about 25 with lambs. If the agent does not do something the reservation will be over run.

The wind blew hard all afternoon, but the telephone line is still up. Sent in two rolls of film and some that George [Siegfried] developed. Raining.

1915 THURSDAY 1 APRIL

Still raining with the river running, banks full for the first time this winter.

Cut out and made a lace camisole, looks so nice I may make an underslip and wear it for a waist, guess not.

Just got back when Sven came with the mail. The mail is still slow about getting thru from Seattle. The river still up and as it has rained all day, will most likely go higher.

Ordered some groceries and wrote Hal a letter; one came from him to his aunt [Mrs. *She-ste-cop*].

Raining hard. Part of order from Huntley's.

APRIL FRIDAY 2, 1915

Raining, which it has been at all night. The river was up to the foot of the big cottonwood across the river.

1915 SATURDAY 3 APRIL

Clear in spots, but last night it rained hard for about an hour.

April Sunday 4, 1915

Cecil [Jack Ward's sister. Wife of Joe] Pullen gave birth to twin boys this evening [Levi and Charles]. The first twins born in the Quileute Tribe for over 50 years. Cloudy.

Monday April 5, 1915

Got some clams from Mrs. *She-ste-cop* for Mrs. Sult. Read her Hal's letter. Hal made a good showing in the contest with the Tacoma school, he must be quite a wrestler.

Abbie [McKechnie], Frank, and Tealie went up to school and walked back with Nell. Oscar Wahlgren brought Mr. and Mrs. Sult and Mr. Christie down after the clams; they took [some] up [for] Mrs. [Frank] Ackerly[58] too. Cloudy.

Cecil, Joe, Levi, and Charles Pullen.

April Tuesday 6, 1915

Not much mail. Two pails of candy. Nell waited for the mail; the proofs of her pictures came. I like the one taken standing. I wrote Lucille, hope the doctor brings her in [from hospital at Port Angeles] with him next Sunday when he comes.

1915 Wednesday 7 April

Blew hard during the night, looks like Floyd would not get here very soon. Not if this stormy weather keeps up. The ocean has been rough for two days.

Frank's fingers kept her awake all night. [Jack] Rainey down after supplies for the camp up the Dickey. Joe Leyendecker in, he is going to the camp to work. Clears up once in a while. Had a chicken for dinner. Nell stayed and Tealie went home with her. Blowing pretty hard again this evening.

April Thursday 8, 1915

Clear in spots. Tealie came up with Nell when she went to school. Walter brought the mail. The dept. sent in an advertisement for new bids to carry the mail between here and Clallam Bay. The fact that they entered into a contract with [Walter and Charles] Palmer's a year ago does not seem to trouble them much. Wonder what value Uncle Sam puts on his honor, a few cents seems to cover quite a lot of it. How can any government teach honesty when it has none itself.

Johnny Hermanson brought down eight dozen eggs, we will live on them for a while now. The only thing that interests me in the daily news is the day advice's regarding the submarine F-4 [that exploded off Honolulu]. Cloudy, the sea calming down quite fast. Floyd may make it down tomorrow.

1915 FRIDAY 9 APRIL

Showery. About nine Clara Smith called up from LaPush and said she and Stella were there, the *Rhody* lays behind James Island. Morton [Penn] will go down towards night and bring them in. The girls walked up. The *Rhody* did not get any farther than the cannery; the tide was not high enough.

Nell's portrait

APRIL SATURDAY 10, 1915

Wrong lock sack sent down. Cloudy. The *Rhody* did not get up the river till about ten o'clock. Johnson Black, Robt. Lee [*Ta-thlo-bisk*], and Morton Penn helped unload, all here for dinner.

Sven and Howard Hayes came with the mail. I went to Forks with them. Mrs. Sult did not go to the Hall. The Indians gave a drill, sang yell song in Quileute, played basketball and winning team played a team from Quillayute Prairie.

APRIL MONDAY 12, 1915

Raining. Ed Walker brought down a load of mail. Have not heard from the order to Spauldings yet; looks as if it might be lost. Quite a bunch of goods for the Indians. C.C. Hobucket, Talcus Eastman, W.J. Jackson, and Agnes Black. I better keep a record of who receives packages from Washburn's [store] as it seems to be a habit for the mail from Neah Bay to the Indians to get lost. Went to the cannery with Nell and stayed all night. Had a great time. Had bear meat for dinner.

Robert Lee on right

April Wednesday 14, 1915

Clear. Got up early so Nell could get to school.

W.F. and Morton [Penn] went to the ranch, took both the horses. Snokums had a pack too. I had baked six pies and a cake. W.F. took the cake, and it looks like there would be pie for the yellow dogs.

Abbie [McKechnie] and Frank went just after breakfast. Abbie was going to bake bread for sandwiches. I am going to try my luck Friday. Just because I want good bread it will be no good. Nell had some supper here. Clear and cool. The weather is great. Intended to have beach party tonight, but Eb wanted it put off till Saturday night so he could go.

1915 Tuesday 15 April

Clear, a lovely day. Do not know why I got up so early. Had my breakfast and called Billy [Hudson] asking him to send Susie up [if Susie is Billy's wife, this is Demer.] She only washed the clothes that were down stairs [and] she washed the dishes.

Ray Palmer and [nephew] Ernest were down with parcel post;[59] had dinner with us.

April Friday 16, 1915

Clear. Susie came before I was up. Yeast was fine and bread turned out good.

C and M [Curtis and Miller] photo of Washburn's

Billy Iverson down with Christie, Billy Collins, and the new driller. All but Billy I. went to LaPush. Billy worked on the gas engine, works all right. Had him come.

1915 Monday 19 April

Clear by times, foggy.

The Indian boys are across the river again this evening fishing for trout. The older Indians used to fish in the same place when they were youngsters. Clear and cool, foggy on the prairie.

1915 Wednesday 21 April

Clear. Frosted last night. Theo Klahn and Charley Hagadorn down after oats. Sent up two sacks for Earl.

[R.W] Remp, Jake [Hahn] and Henry Marshall down. Marshall took supplies up to Little Prairie. Jake is going to run a pack train from there. Grader down. Rixon, Henry, Cliff, and Al down in Rixon's car. Mr. Rixon came in and had some huckleberry pie and coffee.

Young fisherman

Beach party

APRIL THURSDAY 22, 1915

Clear, slight fog for an hour or two. Tealie washed up the white skirts that she and Nell wore to the beach party.

Lew Shumar [Louis Shomar] and Van Welch in from Angeles in Shumar's car. Took the boat and rowed across the river, then walked to LaPush. Shumar thinks our roads are great. Well, they are an improvement over the Angeles roads.

S.G. up to wait for the mail, which was some what late again. Happy and Ed down. Mr. and Mrs. Keene, the children and Leona came up in a canoe. S.G. changed his opinion of Leona some. Doris [Keene] gets cuter every day, she is not so pretty.

Have not done much reading late, too much headache. Ordered some Mary Jane's with rubber soles, if they do not get here pretty soon will be wearing out some of my old shoes. Clear.

1915 FRIDAY 23 APRIL

Clear. Made some blueberry pies the other day and they were fine. Tealie and I packed a bucket full of lunch and potatoes, Morse's did the same and we met on the lower end of the island, made a big bonfire, had baked spuds and sand in most everything we ate. The girls got five trout and tried to roast them over the fire; two fell in.

Road between Mora and LaPush

George came and then we did have a fire, he and Nell chopped down a tree. S.G. went home early, while Mrs. Morse was the best wood rustler that was present. Cloudy all evening but cleared up just before we came home.

April Saturday 24, 1915

S.G. went up and waited at Eb's for us.

Tealie ironed up her clothes and Nell's. John [Hermanson] called up asking if she [Tealie] wanted to go to Clallam to a dance, he came shortly after dinner and wanted his mail proposal bond signed.

George came up to fix his car, asked me to go to Forks with Mrs. Morse and the girls.

Walt in early, not much mail. Took my heavy coat as I noticed Mrs. Morse had on rather a light coat. Wore my green sweater and cape. Met Al with a crowd just leaving for Forks.

Took Mrs. Sult along and went over to "The Toggery." I bought Tealie three silk waists and crepe cloth for to make a dress, a scarf for Lucille and a hat for Nell and I. It was pretty cold at Quillayute coming home. Mrs. Morse wore the coat. Nell gave up the wheel after nearly wrecking us.

The *Pearl* being towed in by the *Albert*

1915 SUNDAY 25 APRIL

Mrs. Rixon came down and took Margaret Orrett up with her. They went down to Ferguson's for a while, we caught up with them near the forks of the road when we were on our way to church.

Frank Buttolph [Batalph] and George S[iegfried] came down and went to the cannery. I went down after the office closed at noon.

We all came up and went to Forks. Clear.

APRIL MONDAY 26, 1915

Clear. The river covered with jumping trout; the Indians did not fish today. Clear and not quite so cool.

1915 TUESDAY 27 APRIL

Clear. Earl [Wilson] got up and kindled the fire. The *Pearl* still outside. All hands to the beach. Earl went to the cannery and fished. A heavy west wind blowing and a nasty sharp sea coming up. The weather clear and cold. Got supper for Guy [Lesure] and Mike, Earl stayed at the cannery.

APRIL WEDNESDAY 28, 1915

Cold. Still [too] rough to get the *Pearl* in. Earl going home and will come back when the boat gets in. He took the turkey hen that has 14 little turks up home; did not lose one of them. Mary says he will camp in the hen yard now. We had quite a time catching the old turkey, Earl pulled out all her tail feathers.

Scow bringing freight from the schooner *Pearl* at Mora

Cold and clear, but the ocean is getting rougher every hour, as long as the wind is in the west the *Pearl* is safe behind the island, but if it changes to the south she will be up against it.

Got supper for the boys and they went to LaPush to go aboard. Hope they will get in tomorrow but not much chance, the *Pearl* runs on a breaker too much.

Cold, still clear, wind still rising.

1915 THURSDAY 29 APRIL

Blew a gale during the night. One of the Indians up and said that the *Pearl* had put to sea, and she would sure be wrecked as the sea was mountains high and sharp as a knife. The Indians are all on the hill watching and crying for the *Pearl*.

Sally [Black or Williams] called up and said she was coming back. W.F. and George went down. Guy and Mike came back with them. Guy cut vein in temple with flying glass. Mike cut bad on the wrist. The windows in front of cabin all smashed; fire buckets gone, oil tank also. The cabin filled with water from giant breakers. The boys going to sleep on shore as storm is still raging and there is nothing they can do on board.

Group of Quileute carrying canoe

April Friday 30, 1915

W.F., Guy, and Mike went down to see about unloading. The sea is nearly as bad as yesterday. Weather reports wind as being 100 miles an hour at Cape Reeves. Going some even for the Pacific.

I took my camera and went to LaPush in the evening; it looked so stormy thought I would get some good pictures. Heavy bank of clouds to the south, hope the wind does not change as the *Pearl* will be in bad shape if it does.

Pearl and scow

1915 Saturday 1 May

Windy yet. Joe Pullen unloading the *Pearl*. The Indians, for the first time in three years, packed their canoe load up from the river.

May Sunday 2, 1915

Clear. W.F. went out on the *Pearl*. I went to the cannery for my dinner. George [Seigfried] was down.

1915 Monday 3 May

Clear. George took Nell to school. Last night I invited Mr. and Mrs. [Charles and Mary] Sult and the dentist down, also Ray [Palmer] and Frank [Batalph]. I intend to

Pearl heading out

have a bonfire on the island tonight. Mrs. Sult and Mrs. Terry came down with Al [Fletcher], all went to the cannery for the day. George brought the Dr. and Mr. [Fred] Terry down, I went back with him when he went for Ray and Frank. We made Frank think Esther was coming. Frank spilled all the strawberry jam on Ray. Al and Nell made the fire and baked the spuds. Nell and the Dr. nearly made themselves sick eating salad. Mrs. Sult and [the] Terry's had to go about 12 o'clock, Al took them. George near cooked all of us by making up a big fire and then expecting us to set close and have our pictures taken. Everyone seemed to enjoy themselves. Clear.

1915 WEDNESDAY 5 MAY

Got Nell's breakfast, Frank [Morse] and George [Siegfried] up too. Frank had to hurry home. George came back from school just as Tealie was eating her breakfast. Susie came to work and had breakfast, Al got up about ten.

I baked a cake and Tealie and George made the frosting. George spilt sugar all over the stove. Had dinner when Nell came from school. George, Nell, and Ross in one car, Al, Frank, Tealie, and I in the other went to Forks. Had two blowouts on the prairie, fixed them. One of them went good up by the Fraker Place, went in on a flat tire. We all came back with George about nine. The girls went home. Clear.

1915 FRIDAY 7 MAY

Lloyd's birthday — 20 years old [1895]. Clear. Walt after the mail about 8:45. Brought in 5 cases Del Monte tomatoes, came by freight. Will have to see who made the mistake in shipping. Walt says the other five are at Forks. The four cases of vegetables are also on the way, but they are coming by mail.

1915 THURSDAY 13 MAY

A nice day. Ironed all day, did a three weeks ironing. Made a veal loaf. Called up Mrs. Morse and asked them to supper. Mary Hutsell went on home, as Mrs. Morse does not need her now that Lucille is home. Harvey and a picture man at LaPush. Dr. Woods on the mail, he always comes unexpected. Got two dozen eggs from Mrs. Ed Smith. Tealie went home with Lucille. The wind blew hard today. Cleaned up my room, it needed it. Colty ran away and left Snokums. Raining.

Mr. Smith with chicks

MAY FRIDAY 14 1915

Clear at times. Made up mail and got breakfast. Arthur [Howeattle] was up early to mail a letter.

Tealie took [in] the waist of her new dress. I made a Lady Baltimore cake and it was dandy. Made a gold cake too. Fan [Morse] came home with Mr. Marshall—two woodcutters came for S.G.

1915 SATURDAY 15 MAY

Lucille up, not sure she can go to Forks tomorrow because of the ball game. George and Nell came in from Angeles about ten. George was tired, had been up all night. We took Cile up to Gretta's as Eb is in Angeles. It was raining hard. I made up a bed and put George to bed as soon as we got back. He was so tired that I do not believe he stirred all night.

Nell got a new hat and two new skirts, a navy serge and a white poplin. The serge is a dandy, box plaited with a shirred top, and it fits Nell fine. I do not like her hat so well. She got two caps, one each for herself and Tealie.

Blowing and raining hard. A social at Forks tonight.

MAY SUNDAY 16, 1915

Sun shining, you would think it never rained. Tealie went to Forks with Grader as did a lot of the Indians. Grader altered Snokums. Nell and George went to Forks, took Henry Klahn and Sherman Parker up, came back for me.

Lucille driving, Nell and George in back

Just as we got to the turn we met a Pierce-Arrow and a Packard on their way to Mora. Bill Hudson was up with a canoe for them.

MAY TUESDAY 18, 1915

Rainy. Tealie and Nell went to Forks. George brought Nell home, but he did not stay. This is Nell's last week [teaching] in [Mora] school and I imagine she is glad. Next year she goes back to Bogachiel.[60]

1915 FRIDAY 21 MAY

A good day. Baked bread, which was good for a wonder. My bread is good when I make it up in the evening.

Tealie baked a chocolate cake and cooled potatoes for salad and made the salad dressing for her share of the lunch tomorrow night. We also cooked half a ham. I fixed my grey flannel skirt, it has always been so bulky at the waist and I am fleshy enough at best. Had quite a time making frosting. My cake was alright but the frosting was too hard. Clear.

MAY SATURDAY 22, 1915

Clear. Nell and myself are going to get the lunch ready and send it up with Walt. Mrs. Hicks came in with Wesley. Tealie is at Forks; the girls are cleaning up the hall for tonight.

1915 SUNDAY 23 MAY

Clear. Everybody out Sunday, the popular day. The Neah Bay's did not come to play at LaPush, so the Forks boys came down. W.F. took them down in the powerboat. Forks beat.

Stayed at home all day. Walt and Frank let the cake get out of the box and break up, then they had to eat all they could hold, and hid the rest under a log. The girls took in $41.

MAY MONDAY 24, 1915

Tealie stayed all night at the cannery, but I came home. The tide was so high that I had to climb over the jam by the camping place. A log turned over and I got good and wet. Went to bed as soon as I got home. The tide was unusually high and it was raining to beat the band.

Rock cuts at Lake Sutherland

MAY FRIDAY 28, 1915

Eb and Joe Marsh here. The general manager for Fisher Bros. and three others in, in a Ford. W.F. took them to the beach. The *Jean* unloaded. A nice day and it was appreciated after the rain.

MAY SUNDAY 30, 1915

Rixon's just ahead of us from the rock cuts. Margaret [Orrett] along. Mr. Rixon went in on the *Betty* [Earles] and Mrs. Twilleger [Terwillegar] went with us. Anderson's and myself took in Sequim Prairie and Haggith's thoroughbred pigs. Sequim and the Dungeness bottoms look like farming paid in that section at least. Some of the finest farmhouses I ever saw. Sequim has a high grade of milk stock — and irrigation. Stayed at Anderson's. Clear. Today my first trip on the ferry. Calkins of the Milwaukee [Railroad] down.

1915 MONDAY 31 MAY

Clear. Clouds around Mt. Angeles. Lloyd up. Says Floyd [Johnson] and Stella were married yesterday.

Bob Polhamus was hurt pretty bad when he put his new Overland over the bank on Lake Sutherland, do not think he will live, is bleeding at the lungs.

Went down and saw Stewart. Marshall came just as I was eating and I had to go. Took some pictures of Bob's car when we passed [Lake Sutherland]. Took a few views along by the rock cuts. Am going to walk over that road some day and get views, that is the only way. Got good and tired before I got home. Met Nell, George, Lucille, and Tealie at the Mora schoolhouse. Mrs. Rixon was down and went to David's [Hudson] after berries.

JUNE TUESDAY 1, 1915

Rainy. New mail contract went into effect today [to Jake Hahn and Al Fletcher]. Jake broke down and George [Siegfried] went out and got the mail. Lucille, Frank, and Tealie went to Forks with George and Nell. Mrs. Bob Anderson lost her bloomers while she was playing basketball, must have been quite a show.

Car on new road

Harvey's black bull makes regular trips to the prairie – and back when Harvey leads him. The river has few terrors for the old black devil any more. He will go into beef quicker than intended if he is not careful.

JUNE THURSDAY 3, 1915

Foggy in the morning. Made a map and timetable for trip from Angeles to Mora. Made up and mailed monthly P.O. reports. Not much mail came in tonight. Made up part and left letters for the morning. This good weather gives one the wanderlust. Orretts are sending out lots of mail, they must be going to move, school will soon be out. Set yeast and made up bread to bake in the morning. Wrote some long overdue letters.

1915 FRIDAY 4 JUNE

Clear. Called up Nell and asked if she would go to the ranch with Tealie and I. We left about eleven. Found all kinds of strawberries and while I got dinner Nell and Tealie got berries ready.

Went to the beach about six but the tide was in too far so after taking a few pictures we came back up to the house.

Nell and I ate more berries and then we went and picked all there was, which filled two big kettles. I had to get up and put the dogs out, Teddy got so noisy. Read awhile.

Nell and Tealie on the beach at Taylor Point

JUNE SATURDAY 5, 1915

Made a mistake and got up early. The girls got up about nine, when I had breakfast ready. We all set around and read till about half after one when we hit the trail for home. Found the mail had beat us. Had to take the boat and go back after Teddy, he refused to swim.

Three cars came in and went down by the island where they camped. Two of the women came up and wanted to get drinking water; told them we got ours from the river.

Charles Howeattle up for the first time this year with his boat, it seems fine.

W.F. took K.O. [Erickson] to the cannery. He came down with Ivor and John Hilstrom.

Too foggy for pictures.

JUNE MONDAY 7, 1915

Tealie came along and had forgot my camera so I had to go to the ranch without it and of course tide and weather were ideal for beach pictures.

Picked 14 quarts of berries. My feet were rather tired so I sat and read. Did quite a bit of writing and answered lesson No. 8, wonder how near it is correct. The weather is fine, would be great to camp out.

The last of the three cars went out this morning, wonder who they were and where they came from.

Clear.

View South from Taylor Point

Taylor Point cabin

1915 Tuesday 8 June

Clear in spots. Picked over and canned the berries, there were six quarts of jam besides what fresh berries I will take home. Cleaned up the house and started home about 5:15. We could hear Laddie barking when upon the first hill.

W.F. came over and got me. George and the girls went to Forks to the basket ball game, all stayed here.

Good weather. Took me two hours to walk up to the river.

1915 Saturday 12 June

Cloudy — Misty at times. About eleven a Mr. Henry and wife with their two little girls came in from the lake and walked to the beach, had David bring them back in a canoe. I got them a lunch.

David [Hudson] brought some lettuce and a pail of berries up. Al got in about eleven with the mail. Tealie went to Forks with George and Nell; they are going to Jake's [Hahn] wedding.

I left for the ranch about 3:30, was on the second hill at 6:15, at 8 I was at the ranch with the fire kindled and 8 qts of berries picked. Was pretty tired and stiff by bedtime as I was too warm to go picking berries right after a walk. Cloudy. Can see the [Destruction Island] light. Eb got back today. The *Jean* did not get in the river, broke down in the surf. Went back to Destruction.

June Sunday 13, 1915

Cloudy. Did not sleep well last night, must of caught some cold last night. Finished picking strawberries this morning. Had to recook the ones I put

Canoe across from LaPush

up a week ago. They had not spoiled. Got eight quarts in sugar getting ready to cook. Read some; have got to clean up the big table before it walks off. Took some pictures and packed down a basket of wood from the hill. Was going to the beach but the tide did not go out far enough till too late, so I finished picking over the berries. Found the Crisco gone, someone has been helping themselves. Feel like sewing but better not. Sun shone for a while this afternoon. Cloudy. Warm all day.

1915 MONDAY 14 JUNE

Woke up early but it looked so foggy that I could not get any pictures, so went to bed again. About noon the sun came out and everything was clear as a bell, but the tide was in too far then.

Put up some more berries, read and straightened up the big table. Sorted the magazines. Worked the rose on one side of the skirt waist, looks a lot better now that it is finished. Would like to know what makes the cook stove smoke all the time. The pipe is straight and it does not seem like that will stop it up. The phonograph is so dirty that it will hardly run, no wonder, the cover is always left off. Clouded up again.

JUNE TUESDAY 15, 1915

Foggy, got up early anyway. Waited til afternoon to pick berries, as it was so wet. Finally had to get out in the wet and pick them anyway, got about 12 quarts. Put them in two big coffee cans and packed them to Mora. Sent one can down to the cannery.

Tealie, Nell, Frank, George, and Jean went to Forks, came back here and stayed. The girls took Jean down home with them. Had to get supper when I got here – clear. Susie finished the washing.

1915 Wednesday 16 June

My feet bothered so all night I could hardly sleep. Got breakfast for the crowd and made up the mail. George took the mail up about ten o'clock. George and Nell are going to Angeles to take Mrs. [Kate] Siegfried out.[61] Nell insists I shall go too, but I do not think I can afford it. George came down and said there was a new citizen at Forks at Walt Palmer's – that is, was going to be. [Elsie Palmer born on this day].

Clear.

June Thursday 17, 1915

Nell, George, and Frank went to Angeles. Mrs. Siegfried walked to Forks this morning, fell off a log and got all wet in the creek. She was worn out and drenching wet when she got to Forks.

Went over and visited the new baby girl at Walt's, Bertha somewhat tired out, but the baby is fine and healthy. Stayed at Mrs. Sult's. Clear.

June Saturday 19, 1915

Clear. Tealie scrubbed and swept. Ned here for dinner. Used the last of the old potatoes. David [Hudson] up with a lot of berries and vegetables to send up to Forks with the mail. Brought a lot for us. The berries look pretty good. Got a letter from Miss [Sadie] Poling. Her letters are always enjoyable to me. Also hear from Mrs. Reagan, the first letter for some time. They are both well. Mr. Sult came down with Al when he came with the mail. Gave Mr. S[ult] a cake for the Mrs. Made a sponge cake, did not make much of a success baking it. Johnny Smith brought me two dozen eggs. Mary was down. The two quarts of cream was tainted. Clear. Tealie went to the cannery.

June Tuesday 29, 1915

Wesley's down. Susie here and washed the bed spreads for Mrs. Sult. George went to Forks about noon intending to take up the spread but they were not dry, sent them up with Jake. Wischmeyer came in with a couple of strangers. Clear, and warm. Some little turkeys on the island. Had sole for supper. The river is full of them.

Tealie in shepard check skirt, with Frank Morse and unknown

1915 WEDNESDAY 30 JUNE

Feet ached all day, are peeling off. Clear and hot. Finished Tealie's white serge coat. Like it fine. Tealie got a nice piece of shepherd check at Forks Sunday. It will make her a nice suit.

Called Frank up right during the hottest part of the day and told her she could have the three yards of serge left if she would come up right away and sure enough she did. Intended to give it to her anyway but wanted to see if she would come. Ozette special here.

Tealie got her ironing done. It was pretty warm yesterday and today to keep a fire. Keene's, Leona, Farwell, the Morse's and ourselves had a bonfire on the island. Keene's borrowed S.G.'s canoe to go home. I made two attempts before I got home. Tried out on the bar and the water was in the way. Wischmeyer, [the photographer] was at the beach all day. Clear, warm, lovely moonlight. Tealie went to Forks.

JULY THURSDAY 1, 1915

Clear and too warm for comfort. Hot weather hits one hard when there is about two days in the year.

Wischmeyer went to Forks with the two he came in with. Lucille and Frank up. Cile took home her white serge for her coat. The *Igniter* came on the mail.

Tealie in shepard check skirt

1915 FRIDAY 2 JULY

Nell and George went to Angeles. Foggy this morning. S.G., Mrs. Morse, Cile, and Frank went to Beaver Lake with Willoughby fishing. Cleaned up my room and then got lunch. My feet were quite feverish all the a.m.

W.F. took Colty and Laddie and went to the ranch. Jim Clark and Alfred here in Louise's [Clark] car. Joe Leyendecker and one of the younger members of the family here this evening, just came in from camp. Mr. Ferguson also home, he came by the way of Clallam [Bay].

JULY SATURDAY 3, 1915

About eleven last night Louise, George and Nell, and a third car came in. Nell came to the door and said it was Al with a truck load of mail. Nell let him in and then went on down home.

Garde' of Pickard — Garde' here with a crowd.[62] They went back to the lake after going to LaPush. I telephoned Ovington's [resort at Lake Crescent] for them. There were five Seattle cars in. Willoughby's went to Ferguson's. Another car came in late and went down to camp.

Sitting room at Ovington's camp

"Sweet and Low"

[Based upon the caption on her photo, they are probably performing a dance à la Isadora Duncan to the song *Sweet and Low* written by Lord Alfred Tennyson and music composed by Joseph Barney.

Sweet and low, sweet and low,
  Wind of the western sea,
Low, low, breathe and blow,
  Wind of the western sea!
Over the rolling waters go,
Come from the dying moon, and blow,
  Blow him again to me,
While my little one, While my pretty one,
Sleeps.

Sleep and rest, sleep and rest,
  Father will come to thee soon;
Rest, rest, on mother's breast,
  Father will come home soon;
Father will come to his babe in the nest,
Silver sails all out of the west,
  Under the silver moon;
Sleep my little one, Sleep my pretty one,
Sleep.

(Lord Alfred Tennyson, "The Princess: II - Sweet and Low")]

Forth of July at LaPush

1915 SUNDAY 4 JULY

Made out P.O. Report. Clear. Two Seattle cars in, turned right back. A Townsend car reported 10 more. Sent word to Billy [Hudson] to come up, maybe some would want to ride, but all walked. The crowd of campers were around about daylight hunting worms to fish, sounded like a dozen youngsters. Judge Ralston was with the Townsend bunch. I took the boat and went fishing about the time the crowd wanted back, they were the nerviest ones that have made the trip. Got five nice trout. There has been some one here all day. One crowd comes and one goes. The campers got twenty trout late this evening. Seem to be enjoying themselves.

Gordon Hobucket came home this evening. Grant and Clara [Eastman] came down and took him to LaPush. Raining.

JULY MONDAY 5 1915

Fog. Campers left about eight. Jake here at 6:30 for his mail, last time it was ten. Two cars came in about ten and the men of the party went to LaPush, left the boat untied. The

Wesley Smith, school teacher at LaPush between 1883 and 1905, was instrumental in organizing 4th of July celebrations.

Forth of July canoe race

women kindled a fire of pickets right in the road, and proceeded to do a washing. There was a small baby along. I took the clothes in and partly dried them over the range, by the time they left it was raining hard.

Tealie and George came about noon, George went to the two o'clock ferry. About three Mr. Kays and party of Dungeness went down to the camping place. I went fishing and lost my tackle, came back and got a new one, but the fish were after flies so I quit. A lovely evening.

1915 TUESDAY 6 JULY

Fog. Got some sewing done. David brought up some vegetables. Chas. Howeattle down with mail and to take back what was here to the Oberlin College crowd at Ozette.[63] Charley says they are a great bunch.

Two cars - (Seattle) the folks all went to the beach, the nicest kind of people.

I went to Forks with Jake and Mrs. Sult; Tealie, and the girls came later. Bertha's [Mrs. Walter Palmer] girl Elsie is growing — Clear — almost frost.

JULY SATURDAY 31, 1915

Foggy most of the morning and quite a bit of the days now, a great deal of hay will be lost.

The beach party will be a family affair as the Forks people have entertainment of their own on hand. The melons and muskmelons came in, also an awful lot of dogs. I packed the watermelon to LaPush. Had our fire right by Keene's. Jim Koenig seemed to have a good time. Leona came home with Tealie and they are going to Forks tomorrow. The river was awful low.

[August 2 through 8 journal entries are recounting Fannie's backcountry trip into the Olympics]

August Monday 2, 1915

Fog. Nell and I go to Forks with George on our way to Hoh. [Prescott] Kalbfleisch and King go to the lake with George.

1915 Tuesday 3 August

Went from Siegfried's to Terry's.[64]

August Wednesday 4, 1915

From Terry's to the camp near the [Hoh] ranger station.

1915 Thursday 5 August

Up to the summit [High Divide].

August Friday 6, 1915

To the Hot Springs and home.

August Sunday 8, 1915

Spent Sunday at home, still somewhat stiff.

Fannie and Nell with packs, head out on hike into Olympics

Nell and George

Around the campfire

Fannie on bridge

Hoh Ranger Station

Camp site high in the Olympics

Left to right: Charley Anderson, Nell, and George at campsite

Nell, Fannie, and George on hike

1915 SUNDAY 15 AUGUST

Clear. Auto club of Seattle expected but did not come. Lloyd brought Tealie and S.G. down. [Clay] Wolverton down.

AUGUST MONDAY 16, 1915

Went camping at the beach today.

1915 THURSDAY 19 AUGUST

Broke camp, Nell has to get ready to go to Bogachiel [to start teaching].

AUGUST FRIDAY 20, 1915

W.F. and Lloyd go to Angeles, the hottest day for three years.

AUGUST SUNDAY 22, 1915

W.F. and Lloyd back.

Camping on the beach. Tealie in hat, Nell against rock, and Lucille

1915 WEDNESDAY 25 AUGUST

Tealie and myself went to LaPush in the evening. Lloyd was down by island to the camp of four fellows from Seattle.

1915 FRIDAY 27 AUGUST

Mrs. Harvey [Adeline] Smith had an auto accident, car turned over; do not know whether she is hurt bad or not. Tealie and Sis [Mrs. Raun] went to Forks. Tealie to take [John] Grader's car to Rixon's tomorrow.

AUGUST MONDAY 30, 1915

Joe and Jessie [Marsh] went home late last night. Joe and Max Klahn came down and made [road crew] camp intending to go to work tomorrow. Ole Deitlefson [Ditlefsen] here with a load of lumber. Rained this morning, the first time for over a month.

1915 TUESDAY 31 AUGUST

Rained last night, but clear all day. Max went up to upper camp, Parker down to fix bridge [Dickey footbridge]. Mrs. Dinsmore [Ida Dinsmoor of Quillayute Prairie] went out on the stage and Ray came in and went to the Rixon's place.

Finished embroidering the nightgown and began on an apron. Felt some better. Henrrich's were here all day. Grader came down and Mrs. Keene, Doris, Leona, and Tealie went to Forks. They will catch the early ferry.

[According to the Port Angeles newspaper, *The Olympic Leader*, Tealie, John Grader, his mother Sophia, and Mrs. Keene and children went to Grays Harbor and Seattle. Since Fannie says they will catch the early ferry they must have gone to Seattle first. Perhaps they also attended the wedding of Nell and George Siegfried in Port Townsend on September 1. It is odd that Fannie does not mention her friend Nell's marriage in her journal.]

Frank, Nell, and Lucille on ferry

Dickey footbridge view to Morse's

Bridge looking east to Taylor garage

SEPTEMBER WEDNESDAY 1, 1915

A hound dog seems to have taken up residence here. The fellows with the canvas boat went back to Wilson's and came down the river. The [road] machine waited most all day for them.

1915 THURSDAY 2 SEPTEMBER

Tourists are getting scarce.

SEPTEMBER FRIDAY 3, 1915

Clear. The Wahlgren boys are falling trees on the new road. Fred [Wahlgren] fell from the springboard and cut his hand quite bad, did it up for him.

1915 SATURDAY 4 SEPTEMBER

Boy at Eb's, Gretta fine [Baby's name Gerald]. Fergusons, McGregor's, Mrs. Burkhart, and Charley Anderson went down the coast going to stop at the ranch. Nell and George and Tule in from Institute.

Frank visiting at Angeles. Mail late, George brought it down.

SEPTEMBER SUNDAY 5, 1915

Went up to see the new baby at the prairie. A new arrival at Ray Maxfield's, a girl, [Ruth Anna]. Tule and George up. Jessie [Marsh] came down with Joe and is going to camp for the first time in her life.

SEPTEMBER TUESDAY 7, 1915

Rained in the afternoon, the road crew went home. Jessie gave me the sweetcorn. Marshall threshed.

Jessie and Peggy camping

Pkg. From Sears, Roebuck. Jean's locket cannot be repaired, have to get a new one.

SEPTEMBER SATURDAY 11, 1915

Grader's crowd got back about ten p.m. Mr. Keene was here to meet them. Tealie said they had a fine time. Sophy came down and took the luggage of the Burkhass [Bucyrus, early name for Dickey Lake] up to the lake. [Chris] Morgenroth and two men here. Quite a few county cars here.

Jessie Marsh and daughter Peggy

1915 SUNDAY 12 SEPTEMBER

Lloyd and S.G. and Frank came in about one. I went down where Jessie and Joe are camped; Peggy wanted to come home with me. Fan and Sherman [Parker] were at the camp for supper. Fan seems to be enjoying herself. Tealie had many tales to tell of her travels. Lucille started to [teach] school [at Mora] a week ago tomorrow. Frank and Tealie took Lloyd's car and went up to school. Afterwards they went to Gretta's. Took a walk up the road to the schoolhouse.

Taylor house

Taylor gas station

1915 TUESDAY 14 SEPTEMBER

Jessie and the baby went up home. Lucille came from school feeling pretty sick. John Grader brought Cliff down. They are going to build this road and fix ¼ mile more near the Solduck Bridge.[65] Jessie went up home to do some baking.

SEPTEMBER WEDNESDAY 15, 1915

Tule did not go to school. Tealie took Lloyd to the doctor who gave him some pills. Good weather. F.W. Parker came to work on the new building at the Dickey.

[The Taylor's purchased their own land and built a store, gas station, and home on the Dickey – see maps on pages 113 & 115.] The newspaper reported:

> "W.F. Taylor, the Mora merchant, will vacate the building that he has been occupying for the last ten years and will move into a new building which he will construct at the mouth of the Dickey River, just opposite the Morse cannery. He expects to move into the new building before the last of September" (PAOL 1915).

1915 THURSDAY 16 SEPTEMBER

Anna and brother down but did not wait for the mail. Dad [Frank Marsh] brought Jesse down to camp again. I made an attempt to reach the whale that is ashore at the old mouth of the river by going down over the trail from the cannery – never again. Tule able to walk around, but not very swift.

SEPTEMBER FRIDAY 17, 1915

Lloyd and I went to Bogachiel. Mrs. Morse went to Eb's with us. Lloyd got pretty tired on the hill part, but was able to eat blackberries when we got to Christensen's. Did not find any apples at Thompson's.

A German by the name of Webber is staying at Siegfried's. He is on his forth trip around the world.

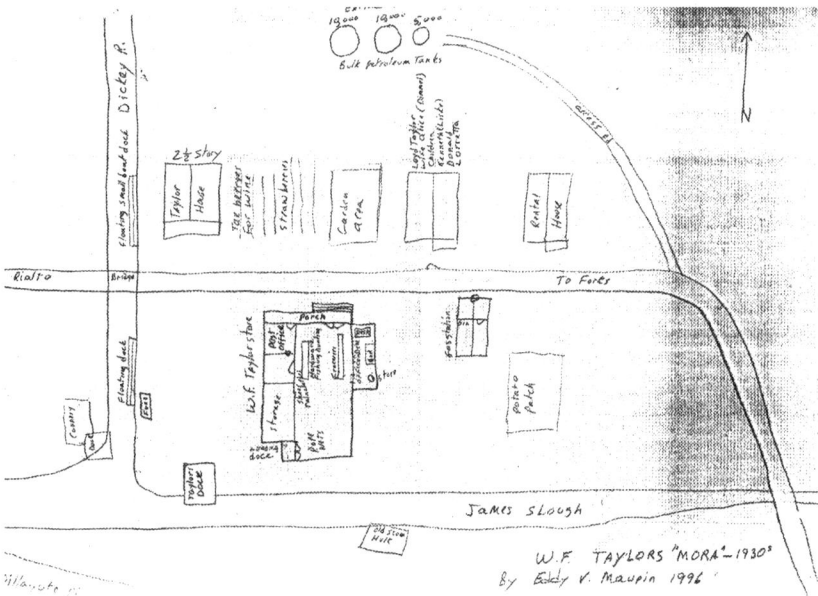

Layout of Taylor complex by Ed Maupin

Bogachiel cable bridge built by George Siegfried

1915 SATURDAY 18 SEPTEMBER

Nell and I went to the Crawford place after berries and parsnips. The berries not very good so went to the Dinsmore [Dinsmoor] place [on Quillayute Prairie]. Nell walked the foot log and I waded the river after jumping on the rocks and sliding in.

SEPTEMBER SUNDAY 19, 1915

Started for home about nine. Frank crossed the [Bogachiel] cable bridge for the first time.

1915 MONDAY 20 SEPTEMBER

John Leyendecker here to eat his meals till the camp is moved. Lloyd put the leather treads on his machine. Billy Klahn came to work. Jessie had a headache all day. That was what she got for going to Clallam to the dance.

SEPTEMBER TUESDAY 21, 1915

Tom Kelly came to work with Grader's team, will have to board him too.

OCTOBER 20, 1915

Actually the store moved to the new location.

1915 SUNDAY 7 NOVEMBER

Raining hard but I made up my post office book and took the dogs and beat it for the homestead. I was 55 minutes to the bridge — 1 hour 40 minutes to the township corner. It was dark in the house when I arrived and then I had to hunt for matches. Came near having to go to the cabin [down on the beach] for them. I was wet and cold and it did not look good. Finally

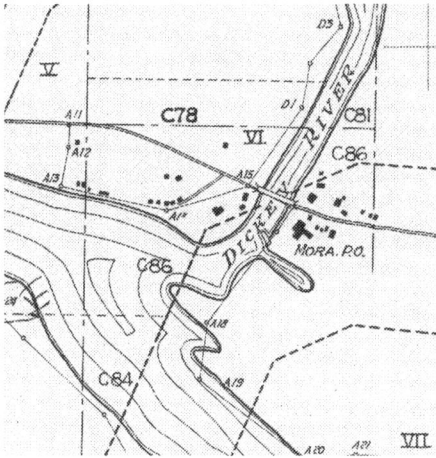
Map of Mora's new locale

found some on the shelf in the kitchen. Made a good fire and cooked supper, went to bed early. Still storming but could see the [Destruction] island light.

November Monday 8, 1915

Clear. Got the fork and went to digging spuds, the blue jays have been here first and spuds are scattering. Have to dig the ground over just the same. The strawberry vines are full of late berries. Rustled a lot of wood to keep two fires going, as long as it is clear I can keep ahead on the wood for the heater. Have two embroidery jobs going, one on a sofa pillow and one on a nightgown. Mammy has a lot of excitement going about the rats under the house. Teddy thinks she is foolish. Storming again, wrote letters.

Thought I heard someone call about dark, thought maybe it was Sis [Roneato Raun] so I went up to see. Guess it was just the voices of the rocks.

1915 Tuesday 9 November

Raining all forenoon. In the afternoon took the basket and went to the hill for wood, did not pay close attention to my business coming down, slipped and thought I had broke my neck for a few minutes. I had about 150# in the basket, so should have been more careful with the head strap. Found it was my back I had hurt, will be good and stiff tomorrow.

During the night saw a sailboat in close, she was running before the wind and going some. Some boat was playing a searchlight on the cliffs when I went to bed. Blowing.

November Wednesday 10, 1915

During the night the sea calmed down, this morning it is like a pond close to shore. Expect Ern will be up, if he does not will miss a good chance. Rainy.

November Friday 12, 1915

Rainy but I finished the spud patch, got 1½ sacks of potatoes for my pains. Had to dig the whole patch over just the same. Did some washing, and have written all sorts of things.

"Part of Giants Graveyard looking north" source of "voices of the rocks"

The voices have talked, laughed and sang every night this week, and at times they sound like harps. If one did not know that it is the rocks and caves and tunnels of the [Giant's] graveyard they would think the air was full of flying fairies.

1915 SATURDAY 13 NOVEMBER
A fair to middling as the Easterner would say. Cleaned up and came up to the office. Tealie had gone to Forks and Lloyd was in charge. Not much mail for me considering it was for the week. Harvey here just ready to go home. Rainy.

NOVEMBER SUNDAY 14, 1915
Clear. Mr. and Mrs. Keene up, both went to the store. Mrs. Rixon and [daughter] Gertrude down, brought some vegetables for Mrs. Dinsmore.

Cabin on beach below Taylor Point

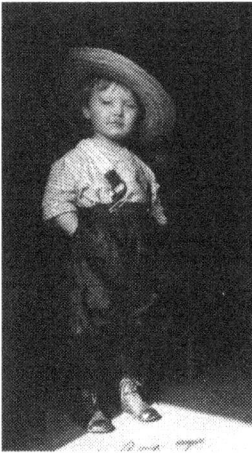

Peggy Marsh

They also made their first trip over the new road to the Dickey. Mrs. K. invited us to dinner. Thanksgiving dinner.

1915 SUNDAY 21 NOVEMBER

Blowing a gale. The *Albert* tried to push the *Rhody* and the wharf over. S.G. got out on the bridge a way and it turned on the side, Bob jumped, and it looked for a minute as if S.G. would go into the river. Took some pictures of the *Albert*.

Last night got the post card pictures of Peggy, sent them right up to Jessie as I knew she wanted them.

Mr. [Captain Albert] Johnson sleeps ashore at the store.

NOVEMBER MONDAY 22, 1915

Tealie and I spent the evening at Smith's; Grandma [Mary Jane Smith] is pretty feeble. Lura proposes a Quillayute Fair; I think it would be a good thing.

1915 TUESDAY 23 NOVEMBER

Lloyd did not get home till near two o'clock. He and Floyd stowed 937 cases of salmon in the forward hold of the *Albert*. Rained most of the day.

NOVEMBER WEDNESDAY 24, 1915

Did not get up till late. John Sailto brought over some hay and put it in the dry house.

1915 THURSDAY 25 NOVEMBER

Thanksgiving and blowing the worst of the year. S.G. sent up a turkey and I cooked it for the men down at the store. Floyd and Mr. Johnson will help eat it, if Tommy gets the rest ready.

1915 SATURDAY 27 NOVEMBER

Rhody and *Albert* left for mouth of river. *Albert* grounded on lower riffle, got off but went ashore on the Muscel Island right in the breakers, was washed over into deep water in shore.

I went to LaPush with Mr. Keene and Leona. Floyd up to Keene's phoning for *Pearl* and *Snohomish*. She is in the open pretty bad, but there is not any sea or wind.

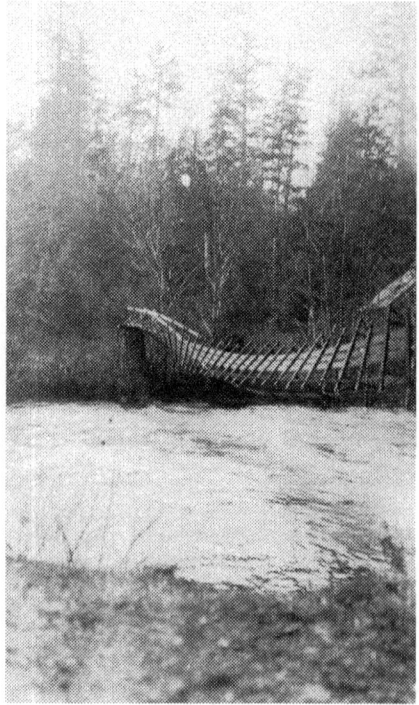

Dickey Bridge on its side

NOVEMBER SUNDAY 28, 1915

During the latter part of the night the wind and sea began to raise. I did not sleep much thinking of the *Albert*. She was in farther, about 200 feet up the

The Albert in the Quillayute River

The *Albert* aground

channel. About ten the *Pearl* arrived, she did not come in as the tide was out. The *Snohomish* turned back at Carrol Island. Heavy wind outside.

Tealie came down for her breakfast. The sea got rougher all the time and by three o'clock was breaking past James Island. The *Albert* turned around on the lines they had to the island, and if the *Snohomish* had come ahead with tackle she could have been kept afloat. The deck load will have to be lightened ashore. Raining and blowing.

1915 MONDAY 29 NOVEMBER

Too stormy today for the *Pearl* to come back. They had a fierce old night last night. The *Albert* is high and dry this a.m. They are taking the cargo ashore on the spit. Alfred down surveying the LaPush road.

NOVEMBER TUESDAY 30, 1915

Calmed down during the night and Guy [Lesure] was here at high tide. Came in. The *Snohomish* not coming to help. S.G. wired McAfee, who could not come as he is without a powerboat.

Dr. Woods on the mail. I cooked two chickens and got dinner at the store for the men. A nice day in spots. Tealie went to Forks with Jack.

1915 WEDNESDAY 1, DECEMBER

Dr. going back on *Rhody*. *Snohomish* lay about 7 or 8 miles off shore. Skipper has cold feet. The men had to row in with the tackle; *Rhody* towed them back, and then went on to Neah Bay. Things are about the same with the *Albert*.

DECEMBER THURSDAY 2, 1915

Rain in showers. The anchors and lines were fixed on the *Albert* so she could be floated tomorrow. I went down and ordered some baskets for [Franklin] Metcalf. At times the wind just raised Cain. Spent recess with Leona and Mrs. Keene.

Arthur [Howeattle] took me across the river and I took five pictures of the *Albert*.

1915 FRIDAY 3 DECEMBER

Lloyd got up and went down early as they want to get the *Albert* off. The tide had been running out two hours before a swell caught her and took her free. She is up in the river tonight for which all are thankful.

Finished my linen tray cloth, it looks fine.

DECEMBER MONDAY 6, 1915

[George] Groffmann down on way to Harvey's place, kind of sore because I did not collect his bills. I am not running a store for him. Went up to school house and got two quarts of cream. Tealie went to store and cooked dinner [Store used for restaurant].

Lucille and Fan up. Gretta is going to take the baby home.

Raining and thundering.

Groffman came down and went to LaPush with some goods.

1915 TUESDAY 7 DECEMBER

The mail is late as Billy met them with the team at Canon Creek. Rained and blew all last night and still at it today. Some of the Indians left the public canoe on this side, so I bailed out the red boat and went after them. Charley Howeattle fed the horse and cow. The river rising. Mr. [Albert] Johnson and [Mr.] Beach came in with the *Rhody*. Johnson tried to butt Muscel [Mussel] Island over. Tied the boats high. It sure rained hard this afternoon. S.G. went to Forks with the mail, going to Clallam tomorrow.

DECEMBER WEDNESDAY 8, 1915

Lloyd got up early and went down to the store. The *Rhody* is tied up at the wharf. The Bogachiel is the highest it has been in two years, while the Quillayute will have to raise two feet to reach the high water mark of last year.

James Island and Mussel Rock (Mussel Rock at upper left)

Quite a little drift running. Water nearly up under the store.

Finished one of the pillowcases, they are not as easy to work as the linen goods.

Still raining, but not so hard as last night. The river is falling fast. Roger Hudson [brother of Theodore] died last night.

1915 THURSDAY 9 DECEMBER
The rain still comes down, but not so as to keep the river up any. Mail in early as Jake went through with the car. *Pearl* and *Albert* came up to the cannery and anchored.

DECEMBER FRIDAY 10, 1915
Clear most of the time, got pretty cold towards morning. The boats went out on high tide. Ed Smith went along. The *Albert's* engine stopped right on the bar and she drifted around so that she had to go out the south channel. I'll bet things were doing on the *Albert* for a minute or two.

1915 SATURDAY 11, DECEMBER
Clear in spots, heavy sea running. Mr. Keene up and mailed Christmas presents. Harvey brought a bunch of cattle across the river, came near

drowning the old black fellow that so persistently came back last summer. Got a sack of apples from him. Mail in early. Tealie went to Forks to the dance. Raining.

DECEMBER TUESDAY 14, 1915

Jake down about 10:30 for the mail. John Sailto up and brought up some hay. Lloyd and the girls went riding, wanted me to go but I had letters to write. Put Colty on the island and she came back up.

Colored post cards came and I sent some to Dr. Newcombe in Victoria [B.C. Provincial Museum], Harry Washburn, and to the Pacific Fisherman. There was considerable mail going out. Clear and cold.

1915 WEDNESDAY 15 DECEMBER

Did not sleep much as my feet were so cold all night. Clear, finished the washing. Clothes not any drier than when I put them out. Clouded up towards night. I took the clothes in so Colty could be in the yard. Ern came in and the *Myrtle May*[66] was unloaded before Lloyd went down. Cold.

DECEMBER THURSDAY 16, 1915

Warmed up, and rained most of the night. Did not get up till late. The sheep got in on Colty's hay. Al down with mail early. I got the machine out in the kitchen and sewed some. Got pictures of Jessie and Peggy taken at the camp and of the *Albert* on the beach. Lloyd and the girls went to Forks. Sent last of basket order to Metcalf. Cleaned out the tank. Rained most all day.

1915 FRIDAY 17 DECEMBER

Rained as usual. Jake [Hahn] down after the mail, went down and took out three boxes of fish. Ern and Roger Comings here for dinner. Harvey down with some apples.

DECEMBER SATURDAY 18, 1915

Still raining. Am drying all my clothes in the house. John Sailto brought Snokums over; the poor cow can now eat and sleep under shelter. Package from Somers came by express. The furs are a set instead of just the muff. Colty was tickled to see Snokums. Ern was up again, too late for dinner. Raining.

1915 SUNDAY 19 DECEMBER

Rain and some squalls. One of the sheep got caught up in the blackberries, took two to get it out. Snokums and Colty are having quite a visit. Tealie went down to the cannery.

Ern Fletcher's boat *Myrtle May*

1915 Thursday 23 December

S.G. got Frank a watch, Nell and George a set of Patrican silver, George Jr. a Shetland pony, Eb a team, everyone presents galore.

Today has been fine, but a heavy sea is running.

December Friday 24, 1915

Rain. John and Jeff came up and got some hay over. It has been a nasty stormy day. Tealie was at the cannery most of the day. Went down and got feed for Colty and Snokums. Morse's had their tree. Jean had a great time. Felt so bad that I had to go to bed early. Ern left for Seattle.

1915 Saturday 25 December

A good day. Went to S.G.'s for dinner. Same crowd as last year. Had a dandy dinner. Came home and found Colty had opened feed room door and had let the sheep in after she and Snokums had ate the grain by the door.

Walked to LaPush alone after the mail came. Tealie went up with George after the mail and did not come back. Had a good time at LaPush and got lots of baskets. Frank and Lucille stayed all night. Ray and the schoolmarm over. Lloyd ran into a stump and smashed a fender.

December Tuesday 28, 1915

Henry Marshall is pretty sick. The Dr. spent a good deal of his time with him.

1915 WEDNESDAY 29 DECEMBER

Cold - Henry Marshall died this a.m. at nine o'clock. The funeral will be Saturday as Mrs. M wanted to wait for his sisters from Idaho.

The Dr. came down and looked at Lucille's throat, she has a well-developed case of tonsillitis. Tealie down to spend the afternoon with her.

DECEMBER THURSDAY 30, 1915

Cile better. Tealie down. Heavy weather on the ocean.

1915 FRIDAY 31 DECEMBER

Clear. Mrs. Keene, Leona, Lloyd, and I went to Forks to the masquerade. Tealie had gone up in the a.m. It was sure cold. Got home about daylight.

EPILOGUE

Fannie's diaries continue sporadically until 1922, but we end here with the following entry, which was the first entry after December 31, 1915:

SEPTEMBER 26, 1917

Much water has run under the bridge since the above was written, Cile's tonalities was a severe case of diphtheria from which she recovered. Mrs. Morse died last November. Was buried Thanksgiving Day.

Cile's stomach operated on the day before her mother died and she is a long ways from well yet.

S.G. has married again. Mrs. Ken Church. The Keene's are in Pipestone, Minnesota at the training school. And last but not least the U.S. is at war with Germany.

Tealie married a Lieutenant McCall in January 1919, but little is known about this marriage. McCall was from the south, perhaps Mississippi, as they lived there for a short time. No marriage or divorce papers have been found; in fact, most people are surprised to hear that Tealie was ever married. Photos of Tealie with the man in the Spruce Division uniform are most certainly Lt. McCall. At about the same time Tealie married, her mother was in San Antonio with her son Lloyd. The Port Angeles paper states that Fannie and Lloyd "returned home Sunday evening. Lloyd, having recovered, returned with his mother on a short furlough" (PAEN 1919) [probably for the wedding]. There are no surviving journal entries for 1919.

Tealie marries Lt. McCall, Jan. 15, 1919

Frank Morse died on May 16, 1921, at the age of 22 from tuberculosis. After finishing High School in Port Angeles, Frank taught school for the Indian Service for one year at Queets and then at Neah Bay. (PAEN 1921)

Samuel Gay Morse passed away on November 27, 1921. The paper said he "never recovered" from the "shock" of frank's death (PAEN 1921a).

On September 14, 1925, Lucille Morse also passed away from tuberculosis. The front page of the Port Angeles Evening News read:

> Lucille Morse Is Dead After Long Lingering Illness
> Funeral services for Miss Lucille Morse who passed away at Snohomish Monday after a lingering illness will be held Thursday afternoon at two o'clock from the Lyden-Freeman chapel. Rev. Duncan Black will officiate and internment will be in the Ocean View cemetery.
>
> Miss Lucille Morse was born at Neah Bay on August 23rd, 1900, during the time that her father, the late S.G. Morse was Indian Agent there. She attended the schools of this city and Aberdeen. Later, Miss Morse taught school at Neah Bay and also in Jefferson County. For the past fifteen years she has been in ill health and she was known for her cheerful disposition by her many friends and relatives. For the past three years she has been with friends in Everett and Seattle.
>
> Miss Morse is survived by two sisters, Miss Fanny Morse of Seattle and Mrs. George [Nell] Siegfried of Forks and two brothers, E.G. Morse of Seattle and H.C. Morse of Bremerton. They are all in Port Angeles to attend the funeral services. Beside the immediate family, Miss Morse has a number of relatives living in this city and Seattle (PAEN 1925).

W.F. Taylor passed away on March 6, 1944.

> News has been received at Forks of the death of W.F. Taylor, 82, former postmaster and merchant of Mora, on the Quillayute river, at Poulsbo last Monday. Taylor settled in the west end of the county in 1908, homesteaded near LaPush, later moved to what was then Boston on the Quillayute river and later to Mora. The National Park Service bought his property at Mora in 1941 and Mr. Taylor moved back to his old home at Poulsbo. Surviving are the widow, a son, Lloyd, and a daughter, Laurel, living at Forks (PAEN 1944).

On January 5, 1966 Fannie Taylor passed on.

> Mrs. Fannie E. Taylor, 92, of Hadlock, died Wednesday at St. John Hospital where she had been confined the past two and one half months. Funeral services will be held at Washelli Cemetery in Seattle at 2 p.m. Friday. Burial will follow at the cemetery. Mrs. Taylor was born Jan. 13, 1873 in Walker, Iowa. She moved to Deadwood, S.D., where she married William F. Taylor. The couple moved to Keyport, Wash. in 1902, and six years later to Mora, Wash. She remained there, and in Forks, until September of last year when she moved to Hadlock. She was a former postmaster and teacher, instructing students at Fort Defiance, Ariz., for five years and at LaPush for four years. Her husband preceded her in death in 1944. A son, Lloyd, died in 1963. She is survived by a daughter, Laurel M. Taylor of Hadlock, three grandchildren and eight great-grandchildren (PAEN 1966).

Laurel M. "Tealie" Taylor, born November 2, 1897, in Deadwood, S.D., passed away on October 28, 1983, in Kirkland, Washington at the age of 85. She resided in Sequim for the past ten years. Tealie was a member of the Forks Post 106 American Legion Auxiliary for 53 years. She worked at Ruel and Vedder Hardware in Forks for 20 years. She moved to Kirkland to be close to her son Ken and his wife Doreen before she died of cancer. Her ashes are interred between her mother and father at Evergreen-Washelli Cemetery.

Keeping someone's memory alive is incredibly rewarding. Some things we will never know. If only we could go back in time and ask the questions that can no longer be answered. As we see the places Fannie visited and meet the descendants of the families she wrote about there is a sensation of her around. The families feel it too, a reconnection to their ancestry. This project has brought much joy and interest in the time period and the lives of some extraordinary people. We hope others will treasure it as much as we do.

Jacilee Wray and Doreen Taylor

BIBLIOGRAPHY

Frachtenberg, Dr. Leo J.

    1916   *Quileute Ethnology; LaPush, Washington*

Jones, George T.

    1974   *Oberlin College Summer Ecology Trip of 1915*. Oberlin College Archives.

Maupin, Ed

    2003 Personal Communication

Minor, Edwin

    1905 Notice to Shakers from Edwin Minor, Supt., Neah Bay, June 14, 1905. BYU MSS 250 Box 1 Folder 1.

    1905a To Luke Hobucket, police, from Edwin Minor, Supt., Neah Bay Agency, December 13, 1905. BYU MSS 250 Box 1 Folder 1.

    1906 To Albert Reagan, teacher, LaPush, from Edwin Minor, Supt., Neah Bay, July 2, 1906. BYU MSS 250 Box 1 Folder 1.

Morse, Bob

    2002 Oral History, May 21, 2002

NARA [National Archives and Records Administration]

    1931 Statement taken by Superintendent Raymond Bitney. Neah Bay Agency. RG-75 Decimal Records 913, Box 45. 40400-1926, File No. 810.

PAEN (*Port Angeles Evening News*)

    1919   January 19, 1919

    1921   May 16, 1921

    1921a November 28, 1921

    1925   September 15, 1925

    1944   March 10, 1944

    1948   July 15, 1948

    1966   January 6, 1966

PAOL (*Port Angeles Olympic Leader*)

    1913   February 14, 1913, page 8

    1914   March 27, 1914, page 4

    1914a May 1, 1914, page 1

    1914b July 3, 1914

    1915   September 13, 1915, page 4

PATT *Port Angeles Times Tribune*

    1909   April 2, 1909

Quileute Independent

    1909 February 4, 1909

Reagan, Albert

    1906 To Edwin Minor, Supt., Neah Bay, from Albert Reagan, teacher, LaPush, April 23, 1906. BYU MSS 250 Box I Folder I.

    1907 To C.L. Woods, Physician, Neah Bay, from Albert Reagan, teacher, LaPush, March I, 1907. BYU MSS 250 Box I Folder I.

    1907a To C.L. Woods, physician, Neah Bay, from Albert Reagan, teacher, LaPush, November 13, 1907. BYU MSS 250 Box I Folder I.

Tacoma Times

    1907 September 6, 1907

Wirick, Eleanor (Toots)

    1995 Oral History by Ed Maupin and Jacilee Wray. May 23, 1915

Woodruff, George

    1907 To Whom it May Concern, from George Woodruff, Mora, Washington, May 29, 1907. BYU MSS 250 Box I Folder I.

Woods, C.L.

    1907 To Albert Reagan, Teacher in Charge, from C.L. Woods, Supt. and Physician, Neah Bay, May 20, 1907. BYU MSS 250 Box I Folder I.

FOOTNOTES

[1] The Quileute name for this locale is Aqt'sot meaning "those who live at the place where there's a riffle in the water."

[2] "Muddy water" in Quileute.

[3] The General Land Office records show W.F. received his land patent for 60 acres in sections 1 and 6 at Taylor Point in 1915 and Fannie received her land patent for 9 acres at the tip of the point in section 12 in 1917 — this is where the cabin was located.

[4] Northwest Coast Indian Shaker religion recognized by the State of Washington in 1910.

[5] Quillayute River and Prairie are spelled differently than Quileute People and Reservation.

[6] The practice was challenged again and again by various Indian Agency Superintendents — into the 1930s according to National Archive documents. In 1931 Hal George wrote in his affidavit that the "birthday parties are potlatches, they "Indian Give" at this party, the birthday party is some excuse for a potlatch" (NARA 1931).

[7] K.O. Erikson, County Commissioner 1906-1912.

[8] Theodore Rixon was chief engineer for a line running from Quillayute to Grays Harbor according to a September 6, 1907, news article (Tacoma Times 1907). In 1908 Rixon was consulting engineer for Clallam County in charge of building the Olympic Highway from the Jefferson county line to Forks (PAEN 1948).

[9] The Ferguson's lived at the headwaters of the Quillayute River; the original homestead belonged to Gus Balch, brother to Frank. Gus was drowned in the Calawah River about 1879. Walter Ferguson worked as a miner, sluicing at Ozette and 2nd Beach. He also cooked for the surveyors and had a trading post at Ozette early on.

[10] According to the Farmers Almanac, the Quillayute Prairie has the worst weather in the entire United States — overcast 240 days per year, 210 of those days it is raining, for an average of 104.5 inches, which is constantly noted in the diaries.

[11] Could be Robert Moran at Rosario Resort on Orcas Island.

[12] Harvey Smith, son of A.J. and Mary Smith.

[13] Harry Maxfield, son of Jessie Maxfield. A.J. Smith and Jessie Maxfield had adjacent homesteads on Quillayute Prairie.

[14] Olympic Leader 2/14/13, p. 8, "Eben Morse is shipping steel heads galore, the Palmer boys taking out 6,000 pounds the last boat."

[15] Floyd Johnson was the son of Capt. Albert Johnson, pioneer boat builder. They built the *Rhododendron, Marion, Albert,* and *Pearl,* as well as scows and barges; their fleet was known as the Pearl Transportation Company. Albert's wife Arilla was a friend of Fannie's from S.D.

[16] Tealie writes on Jan. 20, 1914: I got my sweater tonight. It is just dandy. Mamma says the Q on it stands for Quack. Everyone will be calling me that pretty soon. It doesn't stand for Quack tho, it stands for Quileute.

[17] Harry Maxfield, son of Jesse and Abigail (Abbe). Abbe was Dan Pullen's sister.

[18] Art Wentworth, a homesteader married to Maud Merchant (1879). Maud's mother was Martha Maybury and her grandmother was Mrs. Sam, a Jamestown Klallam.

[19] Horace O. Milbourne had a ranch on the upper Hoh in 1913.

[20] Susie comes to wash and help Fannie throughout these entries. It is uncertain which Susie from LaPush this could be: Susie Morganroth, Susie Black, Susie Jones, Susie Penn, or Mrs. Bill Hudson.

[21] Event from Tealie's diary.

[22] Quileute settlement with several big houses. Hal George's maternal uncle, Harold Johnson lived here, as did Charlie Grader. Quileute word meaning "going up hill place," which could refer to getting the canoe up on the bank. This was a Clallam County port for unloading supplies delivered by canoe to Forks before there were roads to the West End. The location is southwest of Forks on the Bogachiel River, above the Calawah River at Mill Creek.

[23] Harvey Smith had two farms, one on Quillayute Prairie that belonged to his father A.J. and one at LaPush that belonged to his brother David Smith.

[24] Web Jones (Web a had) lived west of the Dickey River on the Quillayute.

[25] K.O. kept a place adjacent to and down river from A.W. Smith's.

[26] "The inside of the Ferguson's home was decorated with animal skins and Indian baskets, mounted heads of elk and deer and bear, and a grizzly bear hide. Myrtle was an avid gardener and had all kinds of plants inside. She grew cactus, some of which were six feet tall, touching the ceiling in the special room her husband had built for her" (Maupin 2003).

[27] The U.S. Government sanctioned seal hunting by the coastal tribes using traditional methods under the 1911 North Pacific Fur Seal Convention. This was an important economic pursuit for the Quileute, as well as a form of status.

[28] March 27, 1914, *Olympic Leader* "Cleve Maxfield has been carrying the mail between Forks and Clallam, taking the place of Charles Palmer who is attending to his spring work on the farm." (PAOL 1914)

[29] Annette Palmer and her daughter Ruth went back to N.Y. Ruth died in 1924 from TB.

[30] Maud was sister to Lizzie Merchant, their Mother was Martha Irwin Maybury. Wentworth's lived below Quillayute cemetery. Their children were Jim, Joe, Bill, Martha, and Arthur Jr.

[31] Mina Smith is Wesley's sister. She lived up the Dickey River and raised five children on her own.

[32] The phone from Taylor Point to Mora was put in April 1909. "W.E. Newbert, who with some of his neighbors will put up a line from Mora to their ranches south of LaPush. At Mora the line connects with the Peninsula Telephone Co." (PATT 1909).

[33] Jesse married to Abbe - children: Cyrus, Annie, and Sadie.

[34] Jesse and Abbe's daughter.

[35] Tenas is Chinook Jargon for child or young, Betty Smith was 4 years old then.

[36] Maxfield's - Ray Maxfield and Gertrude lived about one mile upriver from LaPush.

[37] Possibly Manna, "something of value that a person receives unexpectedly: *viewed the bonus as manna from heaven.*"

[38] Hugh and Marjorie's son, Bob Morse (1916-2006) still had one remaining knife. As a kid he remembered using the knives to cut the "heads off snakes" (Morse 2002).

[39] Probably the Sol Duc burn from Fairholme Hill to Sappho.

[40] Quillayute Prairie School next to cemetery.

[41] In 1913 to get back from Seattle you took a boat to Clallam Bay. In Clallam Bay you could stay at the hotel and order a team of horses for the next day to take you to Quillayute Prairie. There were no bridges, so you had to ford the rivers with the horses and wagon (Wirick 1995:8).

[42] Austria-Hungary at war with Serbia

[43] Mrs. Tyler is Capt. A.J. Smith's daughter Jenny May.

[44] Joe was married to Marjorie Griffith's sister, Jessie.

[45] A good friend of Caroline Rixon's; Ms. Orrett was a niece of Norman Smith and granddaughter of Victor Smith (PAOL 1914b).

[46] Both Fred and Blanche Bartram were teachers at Port Gamble and then taught at LaPush from 1909 when Reagan left until 1911, when they went on to Keams Canyon, AZ.

[47] Marjorie Griffith married Hugh Morse.

[48] Nell teaching at Mora 1914-1915 school year.

[49] Backing up the hill was common as the old autos had their gas tanks in front of the windshield. The steep hills meant that the gas wouldn't flow, as it was a gravity fed system.

[50] Her name is actually *Tsawatsit'sa* or Jenny, married to *Sheshakap* or Jack Hudson. Jenny was Isabelle Payne's sister. Isabelle is Hal George's maternal grandmother.

[51] Fannie's dogs were Laddie, Teddy, and Gyp.

[52] The Morganthaler place might still be found by the piles of rocks that came off the fields. Some of the Morganthaler descendents still live in the area.

[53] LaPush tribal police punished offenders by having them do road work.

[54] The Newbert's moved to Guemes Island in December of 1912.

[55] Lucille was in the Port Angeles hospital when it caught fire on September 25, 1914.

[56] Luther Ford's prairie — one of the first Forks' settler's, he arrived in 1878.

[57] One of the Forks oil wells was 500 feet north of where Art Anderson's wrecking yard is today.

[58] Ackerly's ran "halfway" house at Sappho - probably halfway between Clallam Bay and Forks

[59] Parcel post began here in 1913.

[60] School records indicate Nell Morse taught at Bogachiel until she resigned on November 1, 1917.

[61] Wife of Otto and mother of George Siegfried.

[62] "Mr. Saul, salesman for the Pickard-Garde furnishing house of Seattle is in the West End, combining business and pleasure. He and Max Klahn have formed a partnership and gone into the fur and curio business" (PAOL 1913).

[63] Oberlin College of Ohio came to the coast on a summer ecology trip led by ornithologist Lynds Jones (Jones 1974).

[64] Fred Terry and family took care of the TRH Schmidt house and farm on the Hoh River while Schmidt was operating a restaurant at the World's Fair in San Francisco and the Panama Exposition in San Diego. Schmidt then went back east to visit family and returned with his new bride Jennie in February 1918. They had one daughter, Elsa Schmidt, referred to as *Aha Blip* by the Hoh Indians, she retains that name today.

[65] Sol Duc River Bridge on the Quillayute Road, as the one near the Three Rivers was not built until 1935.

[66] Named after Ern Fletcher's sister, Myrtle May Fletcher Horner

Photographs & Illustrations

Most of the illustrations in this book came from Doreen Taylor and are now in the Olympic National Park collections facility in Port Angeles, Washington. The images with the prefix designation of TAY are recorded in the park photograph collection database. Doreen donated most of the panoramic images to the Museum and Arts Center in the Sequim-Dungeness Valley. These images are cited as such in the list below. The full name of the museum is reduced for space to Museum and Arts Center. We are assuming that the photographs in the two Taylor collections were all taken by Fannie Taylor unless noted otherwise, or unless it is clear they were done by a professional or for a portrait. All other images that have been included in this publication have the origin and photographer properly noted.

Jacilee Wray has served as the park anthropologist at Olympic National Park, Port Angeles, Washington for nearly 17 years. After working for the Washington State Parks, Jacilee joined the National Park Service; her first job as a Park Ranger was at Katmai National Park and Preserve, followed by North Cascades National Park, and then off to a winter position at Chaco Culture National Historic Park — where she met her husband. She went from winter at Chaco to spring at Guadalupe Mountains National Park in Texas, and then both of them took positions at Grand Canyon. Jacilee finished her Master's Degree in Applied Anthropology at Northern Arizona University, Flagstaff. The day before they moved to Port Angeles, Jacilee defended her thesis, *Havasupai Ethnohistory on the South Rim of the Grand Canyons*. At Olympic Jacilee works with the tribes and local communities to document the park's heritage and cultural resources. She was the editor of the intertribal book *Native Peoples of the Olympic Peninsula: Who We Are*, which was published by the University of Oklahoma Press in 2002. Jacilee says that she will miss her research on Fannie Taylor. "It will be lonely after the book is finished, not having to look out for Fannie connections anymore. Well, maybe just a few here and there!"

Doreen Taylor arrived in Seattle in August of 1946. The British war bride of Kenneth Taylor, he and his parents (Lloyd and Alice) were there to meet her at the train station. They took the ferry to Bremerton where Ken's parents lived. In 1951 Ken and Doreen moved to Fairbanks, Alaska where Ken served in the Army at the Alaska Communications System. In 1953 Ken was discharged and they operated a business in Alaska until 1971. Before retirement in 1989, Doreen and Ken lived in Sequim, Washington where Doreen sold real estate. Ken passed away in 1992 and Doreen moved to Virginia to be near her oldest daughter. A few years later she moved to Colorado to be near her youngest daughter, grandchildren, and great grandchildren. Ken and Doreen also have a son who lives in Oregon.

Doreen remembers "one of the first trips I made with my husband was to Mora to visit his grandmother, Fannie Taylor." Ken had not seen her since he had returned from overseas in 1946. There at her house on the river, Fannie and Ken talked for hours, while Doreen slept on the couch. "Fannie was a tall woman with her long gray hair tucked in a bun. She was well read and loved baseball. She could name all the players."

www.ingramcontent.com/pod-product-compliance
Lightning Source LLC
Chambersburg PA
CBHW022024090426

42739CB00006BA/277